'Whatever Happened to GEORGE?'

*After all, it is only our thoughts that separate us
from each other, and a place of everlasting love*

Michael and Lynda Goodwin

BALBOA
PRESS
A DIVISION OF HAY HOUSE

Balboa Press books may be ordered through booksellers or by contacting:

Balboa Press
A Division of Hay House
1663 Liberty Drive
Bloomington, IN 47403
www.balboapress.com
1-(877) 407-4847

Printed in the United States of America.

ISBN: 978-1-4525-7107-2 (sc)
ISBN: 978-1-4525-7108-9 (e)

Balboa Press rev. date: 03/28/2013

Contents

PROLOGUE

It was a Tuesday and it was raining; the kind of persistent drizzle that settles like a mist upon the English landscape, especially in November. The memory of sunny days had long disappeared as the winter had fallen like a giant shadow of distraction, a reminder from the universe that living the English way would give good reason to perhaps feel the loneliness that comes from losing its great source of light.

Yes, the sun was asleep, resting behind a blanket of clouds that would mostly fill the skies until, maybe, March or April, when slowly it would raise its head again and speak softly of awakenings, blessing the silent souls who were now scurrying along the dismal streets with heads bowed ever deep into overcoats of solitude.

Wadsworth Road, in its entirety, is about two miles from end to end, partly comprising a vast network of post-war housing spreading along each side behind tree-planted grass verges and tarmacadam driveways, mainly semi-detached, with the odd, bigger detached property breaking up the monotonous pattern here and there. This type of housing has constituted much of suburban life around the London area since the 1950's and early 1960's. Today, it is still looked upon as 'highly desirable' as city commuters can easily reach the centre of London with a short walk and a fifteen minute train journey from Wadsworth tube station.

George pulled his collar up tightly, the chilly wind biting against his face. He hadn't realised the weather was so grim when he had declined his wife's offer of a lift to the station. Holding his dark brown trilby firmly to his head he kicked a pile of wet leaves, as if shooting a football goalwards, grimacing as the wind lifted them up and blew them straight back at him. He had timed his journey perfectly to allow himself a coffee before taking the twelve o'clock train into London, and as he peered into the distance he could see the dimly lit outline of the shopping centre and tube station beckoning him forward like an oasis of calm, pulling him away from the wind and rain.

With a sideways glance from under the brim of his hat, he glimpsed the busy road; a continuous stream of assorted vehicles pushing up to and beyond the thirty miles per hour speed limit, all trying to reach their destination as quickly as possible. It was never like this when he was younger, he tutted to himself in despair and switched his heavy briefcase from left to right, moving inward to the edge of the narrow footpath, furthest from the road, to avoid the splashes of surplus water as the traffic came in too close. He quickened his step as he approached Atlas Grove, walking hurriedly towards the many bargain shops and down past the bric-a-brac stores, wondering idly how they made a living.

Instinctively grabbing at his hat as a sudden gust of wind threatened to steal it from his head, he tutted quietly to himself again and allowed his thoughts to focus on the meeting. He was comfortable everything was in place inside his briefcase. He had spoken to these people many times on the phone, knew they liked him *and* he was a good journalist with years of experience. His confidence ran high as he marched on - but then faltered a little as his mind considered failure; he hadn't worked for such a long time. Maybe technology *had* left him behind a little . . . . but who could keep up with all the changes happening in today's market?

He shook his head as if to dispel his fears, letting out a sigh of relief as the bright lights of the coffee shop came into view. Opposite the Natwest bank, there it stood, his saviour waiting.

The aroma from the coffee shop drifted out from the ventilation grilles like a magnetic pull of happy retreat from the winter chill. George checked his watch, and entered with a smile of boyish enthusiasm. Once inside, a young person's voice bade him welcome. 'Yes mate, what can I get ya?'

'Well . . . . I, err, just a small cappuccino for me please,' George answered with a modicum of confidence as his thoughts filled with frustration. You see, he could not quite grasp the fact that a simple cup of coffee these days does not exist in the way he remembered from his youth. It was an easy matter then; enter coffee bar, ask for coffee and sit down to drink it. The most difficult thing to wrestle with was how much milk and sugar to put into it. Nowadays, buying a coffee was a bit like taking an examination. Yes sir, is that small, medium or large, caramel, latte, americano, cappuccino, solo? . . . . there should be a course in the art of coffee ordering. Anyway, the lad behind the counter appeared to understand his simple request and set about with his froth machine to make it.

George guessed he was probably about eighteen or nineteen years old, his complexion still showing the signs of early hormonal years, but certainly now improving and like all youths of around that age, managed to carry out his task and hold a mumbled conversation without ever making eye contact with anyone about him. In a dreary, unenthusiastic manner, he passed George's coffee over and took the money, as if his mind was on a different planet, contemplating escape from this cruel life sentence his parents had manufactured for him.

George remembered his own children growing up. Once they hit the mid-teenage years they were gone; lost to a world of TV and music, locked upstairs behind the doors of their respective caves which he could never enter for fear of the green mist taking hold. Months of sulks, silence and secret fetishes; fashion statements; eating disorders and the most peculiar habits, all bringing the day when suddenly, they arrived back on planet earth talking as if nothing had actually happened!

Accepting his coffee, he looked around the brightly-lit room for somewhere to sit, noticing a corner seat by the window was free. He wandered over and placed his steaming white mug on the table and his briefcase under it on the tiled floor, glancing disapprovingly at the shabbily upholstered chairs and peeling hessian wallpaper. Just a moment to return the empties and he would have the best seat in the place. Once done, he gratefully pulled up his chair, settled himself down and blew out a sigh.

He took off and shook his wet hat and unbuttoned his overcoat, and as he sipped at his coffee, started to feel a little calmer, remembering his first ever job interview as if it were yesterday . . . . never believing once that he wouldn't get the job; confidently marching into the editor's office and selling himself without a problem. For a split second he felt the old youthful confidence wash over him and smiling inwardly, he questioned why he felt so anxious today. Maybe it was his age that bothered him. Maybe he spent too much time thinking of failure when he should be positive. That was it! He had to be positive. He had to let go of the stupid notion he was too old. He raised his chin and pulled up his tie, breathing deeply with new confidence.

He relaxed and stretched out his long legs, observing the young business men in striped suits studying the latest figures from pink financial newspapers; non-conformist students with outrageous fashion sense on noisy mobile phones texting out their messages to the world and huddled together in the opposite corner, two young schoolgirls drinking coca-cola through straws, secretly swapping stories and giggling to each other. George couldn't understand it . . . . shouldn't they be somewhere else . . . . working in an office or studying in a classroom? Life had changed. He could see things were different now, with everyone expecting more, with little or no effort. This new generation were not like him, their priorities had changed . . . . and he couldn't understand why.

He sat up straight again, crossing his legs, reflecting on his own younger years; how hard he had struggled to prove himself in the workplace, but how proud he had felt when his ambitions were finally realised and he could successfully provide for his growing family . . . . but it all seemed such a long time ago now. He stared down at his bulging briefcase and pondered on his uncertain future.

Eventually, he raised his mug to his lips again and wiped away the condensation from the steamed-up window, glancing thoughtfully into the bleak drizzle outside, his eyes finally fixing on the clock peering down from the bank tower. Almost five to twelve! A quick glare at his watch confirmed his fear. He gulped down the rest of his coffee, grabbed his briefcase and hat and dashed out to the street. Less than five minutes to cross Atlas Grove back to Wadsworth Road, collect his ticket and find the platform.

Mumbling and grumbling to himself, he increased his length of step, twisting and turning to avoid collision with the shoppers and commuters and swerving quickly around the mothers with pushchairs.

At last, the tube station was within reach, only a few steps to cross the road . . . .

Maybe the car was speeding. George didn't know about that. Just a moment of disaster; a moment of uncertainty and a sigh of breath that uttered a cry to reach the heavens with a plea to take away the anguish of disbelief.

And then, the searing pain of collision, pulling him slowly, towards the darkness . . . .

KNOW WHO YOU ARE

'It is said that man's greatest treasure lies buried beneath his greatest fear. But who has the strength to look?'

An air of musky scent filled the vast recesses of the Library, a scent that seemed to hang everywhere; along the corridors, across the perfectly bound volumes neatly stacked upon the dark wooden shelves, down to the polished lattice of oaken flooring, stretching outwards and beyond where distance could not be recognised by human eyes. Drifting softly through the silence of the great hall, it lingered pleasantly around the perfectly arranged furniture of rosewood and mahogany, melting into the natural light that binds the Library to a place of serenity, a place of peace and comfort, knowledge and truth. Here, a mind could relax within a shelter where time had stopped; a retreat where silence was enough for everything the senses wanted to know.

George sat upright in the deeply upholstered crimson velvet chair, gazing incredulously across the vast, endless area of books. Row upon row, shelf upon shelf, higher and higher to a point of unrecognizable blur; longer and longer, to disappear over the horizon of his sight.

He inhaled deeply. Was it vanilla or jasmine, rose petal or gardenia? For a moment, his sense told him it was his mother's perfume. He remembered coming home from school and opening the door, her scent waiting to welcome him. Then the aroma changed to chestnuts roasting sweetly by the fire, baking endlessly in the ashes and glowing embers of Christmas Eve. An excitement filled his heart with the memories of

Christmas past; roast turkey and stuffing, party hats and his father's sherry he so longed to taste.

It was all here, the smell of the garden in summertime; the lavender and mint, lilac and honeysuckle. Delicate fragrances filled his head with startling memories of distant days full of laughter and good friends, now gone their own way to experience the call of life. He could hear their voices whispering softly in the great silence. How he yearned to see their faces, touch their hands and laugh with them again.

Slowly placing his hat onto the beautifully grained table in front of him and smoothing his hands over his thinning hair, George took another deep breath, his heart pounding to the beat of his childhood years. He stared around, glancing upward again and across to the countless volumes set in flawless position on each shelf.

Where was he? What was he doing in this place of books, sweet smells and memories from his childhood? Why could he hear distant voices from the past echoing through his head, breaking the silence with their calls from yesterday? He was dreaming. In a moment he would wake up . . . . this room *had* to be a dream; a library full of dreams and strange sounds. He could feel his heart pounding, his chest rising and falling to the laboured flow of his breath.

Closing his eyes again, he tried to calm down, but his thoughts now regressed back to the time when he was a young man with great expectations of life to come. He could feel, once again, the freshness of youthful enthusiasm rising inside, and his thoughts shifted to Phoebe; to the first time he knew she was the one.

He remembered touching her hand and holding her close as his heart danced, making him dizzy with desire; walking hand-in-hand across fields of wild flowers, climbing rocks and shouting from the tops of hills. He could see their wedding day, hear the vicar pronounce them man and wife, taste the wine and hear the loving words spoken by friends and family. It was everything he had ever wanted; it was for ever . . . . it was love.

George blinked open his eyes and shook his head, bringing his focus back into the Library, a sense of disbelief overwhelming him. All these experiences happened years ago . . . . but here, he could feel them as if they were happening *now*, within this room of books. He wiped at his eyes and blinked again, desperately trying to make sense of it all . . . . and then, with abrupt realisation, he remembered the accident. He *knew* the car had hit him . . . . but how could this be? Surely it was a dream.

He checked his body and legs, they were fine . . . . he could move . . . . he had no pain . . . . it *must* have been a dream. But he was here, this wasn't home and certainly wasn't a hospital. Again, he clearly recalled the collision . . . . and then the darkness.

He was dead. No two ways about it, George was dead.

But no . . . . he was alive. His eyes told him he was alive. Every sense told him he was very much alive. He slowly gazed around the Library, confusion consuming his every thought.

It was only this morning he had set off to the meeting. This morning he and Phoebe had been together, talking, getting on with life. Only last night they were making plans, so easy with each other, so intense with their grumblings.

George slumped back into the chair as his memories washed over him . . . .

. . . . and the day will come when man will find his heaven, and through his very weakness, a light will shine, a light which will speak of truth and freedom, a light which will bring peace and love to a world filled with fear . . . .

'Oh, I just can't get into this spiritual nonsense!' George tossed the book down onto the bed and turned to Phoebe disapprovingly. *'From my point of view you are either alive or dead. All this gobbledygook about heaven . . . . it's all rubbish.'*

'Now come on George, give it a chance, you've only just picked the book up,' she coughed at him in frustration, pulling the hairbrush a little too roughly through her blonde bob.

'But it's just rubbish. Who on earth has ever come back to tell us they are in heaven? It makes no sense. Don't you think if heaven was so good, everyone there would want us to know about it . . . . if only to rub our noses

in the fact we were missing out?" He scowled at her again with a sigh of boredom. 'Your mother would be the first person back with the gossip!'

'Now that's not fair George.' Phoebe left the dressing-table and climbed impatiently into bed. 'My mother didn't gossip and anyway, she's not been dead that long.'

Her naive reply seemed to fuel the situation. 'What does time have to do with it? Now you're telling me there's a queue for heaven. Oh yes, my mother's dead, but she hasn't quite made heaven yet. No, she's waiting in the queue to see if she's suitable.' His sarcasm spilled over.

'You know I don't mean that, dear . . . . but there are people who have seen spirits. There are mediums who contact dead people for you. You know it happens. Look at my mother's cat; she always said he showed many characteristics of my father.'

'Only because he was lazy and spent most of his day curled up in an armchair.' Again his sarcasm had taken over.

'Well I want you to read it!' Phoebe spoke quite sternly now, pulling the duvet sharply up towards her. 'They say life can become better with a little spiritual knowledge, and I've read the book and there's nothing too difficult to understand in it.'

George turned to face her. 'Let me tell you what I understand. My name is George Eastwood and I'm fifty-two years old. I have a wife and two grown-up children who are a bloody nuisance to me. I have worked all my life and can't see the day when I'll retire because my family always expects more!' He kicked off the cover and strode moodily into the bathroom, the conversation starting to annoy him.

'Oh don't be so stroppy . . . . relax . . . . you do exaggerate.' She snapped back at him as he disappeared through the door, she wasn't standing for any self-pity.

George picked up his toothbrush, glaring at his reflection in the mirror and began vigorously cleaning his teeth. He was concerned about the shortage of money in the household. He was a journalist and things hadn't quite been working out with the company who had employed him, and so a couple of years ago he had decided to go freelance. Times had been hard ever since and he did feel he should take the blame for his actions. He gargled noisily, and after several deep breaths, returned to the bedroom feeling a *little calmer. 'I know. I'm sorry Phoeb, but life doesn't seem fair sometimes and you know I don't like being out of work.'*

'Well . . . . just relax dear; tomorrow it may all be sorted out.' Phoebe was referring to the meeting he had managed to arrange with a fairly big publishing company, and if they liked his work, it would be a big contract which could last a few years.

George climbed back into bed with a sigh. 'Yes, I know, I know,' he smiled at her, patting her leg, yet he couldn't help thinking it was easy for her to say, he was the one shouldering the responsibility.

Tomorrow would be their thirtieth wedding anniversary, and they still held a great love for each other. Not so much a possessive love with great expectations any more, but a comfortable love that maybe, sometimes, was a little taken for granted.

'Anyway,' he smirked, 'forget this heaven stuff; it's just ridiculous mumbo-jumbo.'

Phoebe turned round to plump up her pillow. 'Oh go to sleep, George!' and she switched off the light . . . .

. . . . With a flicker of his eyelids, George's awareness returned to the Library. He was still in this weird place, still caught up in his dream.

Again, he tried to come to terms with his surroundings, staring intensely at the radiant lights moving around the furniture and books; each book with its own glowing effervescent nature, stretching out to touch another light, all dancing together with an overwhelming brightness.

His eyes searched high towards the vast ceilings, all beautifully coloured with assorted mixtures of changing light, shifting and swirling into circles of fascinating tones and brightness. Colours that were somehow deeper and richer than anything he had ever seen before; rainbows of perfection that elegantly moved across the brilliant white walls of the domed cathedral-like chamber.

What was this place? Where on earth was he? Again and again the questions swirled around his head. This was the worrying thing for him . . . . it was nothing like anything he had seen on earth. He panicked a little as his mind fell into the belief he was dead, deceased, gone forever from his world . . . . but death was so final, and he didn't feel finished with life . . . . he could still feel plenty of life inside him.

He filled his lungs to capacity, listening carefully for the beat of his heart, checking his wrist for the pulse of blood coursing through his veins . . . . surely he must be alive.

He mentally tried to retrace his steps, remembering the walk along Wadsworth Road in the wind and drizzle; his drink at the coffee shop, the business men, students, school kids . . . . they all raised memory through his thoughts. But then a blurred recollection of his dash for the tube station consumed him with the dark recall of disaster. He blew out a long breath in exasperation.

He wasn't hungry; he wasn't thirsty; he didn't need anything . . . . he was just totally confused. Was he dreaming? Would he wake up suddenly to find himself lying in bed, at home, with Phoebe beside him?

He gulped as he slowly stood up and began striding purposefully around the table, kicking his legs out in a strange fashion, bending his knees and swinging his arms high into the air. How could he be dead . . . . when he could do all this?

Sitting down in the soft velvet chair again, he rubbed his face. No, there must be a logical answer . . . . but he couldn't think of it at the moment . . . .

. . . . 'George . . . . are you getting up George? I've made some tea.' Phoebe's frustrated tones filled his ears.

'Yes, yes, I'm coming.' He put his head under the pillow and groaned loudly. He hadn't been able to get to sleep until late, his mind had been overactive, and now he couldn't start it working again. Forcing open his eyes, he peered at the clock. Four minutes past nine. He wasn't late, but a pang of anxiety told him he should get moving. Today was important, it was the day of his meeting with the publishing company.

He turned over and stared at the ceiling, trying to focus his concentration on positive thoughts. He knew from past experience that he would rise to the occasion . . . . if only he could wake up.

'George, are you coming down?' again she growled at him.

'Yes . . . . I'm up,' he shouted back, taking a deep breath. It was only eight minutes past, and his train didn't leave until midday, so he would have plenty of time. He rolled over again and stretched languidly, enjoying his last moments, trying to bring a little life to his aching limbs.

At last, he climbed out of bed and walked a little stiffly over to the chair in the corner of the bedroom, picking up his blue checked dressing-gown and slipping his feet into well-worn corduroy slippers. He made his way over to the window and pushed back the curtains, staring blankly at the depressing, wet weather outside and with a shake of his head shuffled wearily into the bathroom to wash his face and clean his teeth. He wouldn't let the weather bother him . . . . not today.

A few minutes later, feeling more alert, he slowly descended the stairs. 'Morning, Phoeb,' he called out as he reached the kitchen door.

'Morning, George, your tea's on the table. Do you want some toast?'

He thought about it for a moment, 'Oh no, not just yet,' and crashed down onto the kitchen chair, taking a sip of luke-warm tea. 'It's a bit cold.'

'Well, it's been poured ten minutes or more, you should have been up.' Phoebe was trying hard to remain calm, wanting this morning to be different, but he appeared to be his usual grumpy self. She resigned herself to the fact he had forgotten. All through their married life George had never remembered birthdays or anniversaries, why would he start now?

'It's fine . . . .' George relented, trying to cool the situation down as he looked out of the window. 'Raining again, eh?' It was more of an observation than a question, and anyway, there was no response. He tried again.

'It's a big day for us today, Phoeb,' he smiled across the kitchen.

'Oh darling, and here's me thinking you'd forgotten.' She turned, her expression lifted. Maybe she had been a little unkind.

'How could I forget, I've been working on it all weekend!'

'. . . . oh . . . . you mean your meeting?' She shrank from the blast of his rejection, her intuition had been correct.

Immediately, George knew he was in trouble, but a timely flash of memory saved the day, like a golden retriever bringing a bone from deep burial. 'Oh . . . . Phoeb, happy anniversary!'

7   'Whatever Happened to George?'

'How could you forget, George, it's thirty years today, you know?'

'. . . . and it's been a wonderful thirty years.' He had to be careful, he knew he could only push his luck so far. All the time she had known him, Phoebe had always been able to see his well meant little deceptions.

She glanced over at him, trying to hide her disappointment. 'I don't know why I bother, but . . . .' she walked quickly across to the dresser to collect the white envelope and small rectangular box hidden in the bottom drawer, '. . . . here you are, George, happy anniversary.' She marched back across the kitchen to place them on the table in front of him and, rising above her discontent, kissed him on the forehead.

'Thank you Phoeb . . . . that's so nice.' George was slightly surprised and pushed back the greying strands of hair behind his ears, a habit he had acquired when he felt under pressure. He tore open the card, and read the beautiful exaggeration of thirty years' wedded bliss. 'That's perfect, it says it all,' he reached for her hand and squeezed it lovingly.

'Well, go on then . . . . open it,' she enthused, feeling a little more tolerant of the situation. He hurriedly ripped off the shiny wrapping paper to reveal his favourite aftershave.

'Oh, that's fantastic . . . . how did you know I needed some more?' She was pleased with his reaction, but George knew he wasn't quite off the hook yet. He searched for escape.

'Well Phoeb, you know . . . . err, you're gonna have to be patient for your gift from me. You see, it's . . . . err, special, and I'm . . . . err, collecting it today, after the meeting in town.' The fact was, he hadn't really expected they would be exchanging gifts and, to be honest, hadn't given it a second thought.

Phoebe smiled inwardly, disregarding his lame excuse. Whenever she had wanted to find a little romance in their relationship, she could rely on him to let her down. She sighed softly to herself.

'I thought we'd eat somewhere in the West End tonight,' he suggested, sensing now, he'd avoided the big hole that moments earlier he had been digging.

'Oh yes, that would be good, if you're sure we can afford it.' George knew they couldn't, but at least she seemed pacified.

Phoebe sat back down and smiled over at him. 'Anyway, I'm so glad you like your present.'

'Yes it's brilliant,' he replied, 'I'll put some on for the meeting.'

'You can wear it on Sunday . . . . the kids are coming round for lunch to help us celebrate,' she tentatively added, hoping this was a good time to tell him. For the last few weeks he had been abrupt with both of them, for no reason at all as far as she could see . . . . but then again, he had been abrupt with everybody.

Now this was a bit of a shock for George's system. You see, of course, he loved his children, but always seemed to him that whenever they made the effort to visit, they either wanted something from him or brought with them a bag full of worries.

'Oh, ... err, that's good, it'll be nice to see them.' He looked up and waited for the catch.

'I think Neville wants to have a chat with you, dear.' Phoebe spoke quietly as she pulled up a chair.

Neville was their youngest; twenty-four years old and finished university earlier in the year with a degree in architecture, but had done nothing since. Consequently, his relationship with his father was occasionally strained and sometimes uncomfortable, to say the least.

George coughed, clearing his throat as he got up from the table and moved to the toaster for comfort. He had to be calm today, with all his energies focused, he didn't need the distraction of his children's' problems . . . . he had enough of his own. 'That should be fun,' he jibed, lowering down two slices of bread.

'Be patient with him George.' Phoebe became uneasy, tightening the belt of her silk dressing gown. 'You know he means well and your opinion is important to him. He's so much like you.'

He couldn't see the similarity himself, but didn't much feel like the aggravation of disagreement. 'You know I'll be fine with him, Phoeb, and help him as much as I can.' He tried to reassure her, but Phoebe hadn't finished yet.

'. . . . and poor Sonia . . . . she's still having trouble with Pete over the split.'

Now they were getting somewhere. Sonia, their twenty-seven year old daughter, whom they had seen married once over, had decided to leave her husband for another man and now found herself floundering in the messy business of divorce. George didn't quite know what she expected them to *do about it, it was her decision which had brought it all about. It was her life, and it was time she took responsibility for her actions. He sighed. At least neither of them lived under his roof any more, bringing their troubles home . . . . unfortunately, they were bringing them on Sunday. But that was that. The toast popped up and he laid it out to butter. 'Do you want some toast, Phoeb; anniversary toast?'*

Phoebe almost smiled at him. 'No thanks, I've had some already.' . . . .

. . . . George stared hopelessly at the lattice flooring, an uncomfortable stab of guilt taking his memories away. Their wedding anniversary . . . . he had all but forgotten, pushing it deep behind his stressful thoughts of the meeting. Had he really been so consumed by his own little world, so blind that he couldn't even write Phoebe a card on their special day? His despair deepened when he thought of the way he had tried to deceive her into thinking he had it all planned out for a surprise later in the day . . . . when all he had been really was thoughtless.

He grimaced, feeling the pain of his actions . . . . what would Phoebe think of him, his deception and his callous attitude towards Neville and Sonia? They were his children and he loved them both dearly . . . . then why was he so abrupt when they wanted him to help them?

He suddenly felt lonely, cut off from his life, he wanted to go back and do it all again, to change the way he had been, the things he had said. But how could he? He felt panic rising, he wanted to shout and scream, long and hard, across the Library, 'I am not dead!'. He wanted to step back in time. He wanted to go home . . . .

George lifted his weary body from the chair and ran his finger under his collar in frustration. There must be something he could do, some way of finding out what all this was about. He needed to calm himself down and think clearly about this situation. He sank down again into the chair, pushing his hands deep into the soft velvet crush. It was real . . . . no doubt about that. He gently tapped his knuckles against the grain of the table. This place was real enough, it couldn't be a dream, he must have been brought here after the accident . . . . but why?

Again he allowed his vision to search high and low looking for an explanation, looking for an escape that would free him from his predicament . . . . but as the cascading light fell softly around his solitary figure, his eyes closed and his thoughts drifted away, pulling him gently back down into his past . . . .

. . . . *Picking up his plate, George headed back towards the kitchen table. He flicked on the portable television as he passed by, and sat down again, turning his chair to face the screen, noisily taking a bite from his breakfast.*

The welcoming voice from the television drew his attention. 'Good morning viewers. Good morning the world. This is Bob Hirshin with the latest BCB world news, and have we got some headlines for you today.' The newsreader looked intently into the camera. 'But firstly, let's move straight away to our roving reporter, Carole Smithson. Good morning, Carole.'

'Good morning to you, Bob,' the reply flashed back through the monitor.

'Now Carole, you're out today in the most southerly province of Reutenburg covering the worst floods the region has seen in forty years. What can you tell us about the rescue operation?'

'Well Bob, I can tell you that so far dozens of people have had to be rescued by helicopter from the torrid floods which have washed away their homes and personal possessions.' She stepped aside to allow the camera to focus on the devastation behind her. 'This rubble behind me is what is left of an old farmhouse and outbuilding destroyed in the night. Rescue teams have been working hard, and at the moment we are not aware of any casualties, although many people are still stranded. All around me people are trying desperately to locate loved ones and helping each other wherever they can.'

Bob interjected. ' . . . . err, Carole, do we expect more storms around the area today?'

'Maybe, is the answer, Bob. The authorities are saying that already, this morning, there has been an additional ten centimetres of rain, which hasn't helped the situation . . . . but the long-term forecast is for clearer weather.'

Bob looked pleased. 'Thanks, Carole, that's good to know. We'll be back with you later, keep up the good work.' He returned his focus to the studio camera. 'Now, let's take a look at the weather for your area . . . .'

'What's going on in the world, Phoeb, it's one thing after another, disaster after disaster?' George looked with concern over his shoulder at her. 'All these earthquakes . . . . floods . . . . famines, why can't they sort this mess out?'

Phoebe peered over the top of her reading glasses, patiently putting down her magazine. 'Oh, I don't know dear, I suppose they are doing the best they can. It's just . . . . well, it's just . . . . we obviously need to stop destroying the planet.' She always seemed to have an answer, making him feel inferior, sometimes to a point of annoying him.

'How can we destroy a planet by digging up a few trees and causing a bit of pollution?' He argued with a mouth full of toast. 'We polluted the skies much more back in the good old days . . . . and the weather was much better then, none of this global warming nonsense.' He devoured his last piece and took a slurp of cold tea.

'Yes, I know dear, but that's just the reason we need to slow down now; the damage has already been done.' Phoebe lifted off her glasses and carefully placed them on top of the magazine. George was always the same, wanting to make an argument out of any conversation. Again, she answered assuredly. 'The planet is delicately balanced, and we are creating an imbalance, which, in turn, is changing conditions on the earth . . . . the weather being one of them.' Pleased with her reply, she attempted to return to her magazine.

George continued. 'Well, I'm sure they could do something to put it right again, with all the technology around these days.' He stroked his chin in contemplation, unable to follow what all the fuss was about. Listening to politicians these days made him feel as if the world was coming to an end, it was always one problem after another, and he couldn't quite understand why . . . . surely things hadn't changed that much. 'You couldn't just do me another slice of toast Phoeb, could you? I'm still hungry.'

Phoebe, again, put her magazine down in annoyance. Sometimes it was like having a child around the house constantly asking questions. 'Yes, go on then, I suppose so.' She left the table a little frustrated and headed towards the toaster, resigning herself to the interruption.

'Thanks, Phoeb, that's good of you.' He took another mouthful of cold tea and turned his attention back to the television.

'Yesterday, at the Old Bailey in London, Judge Stevenson finalised the sentencing of Frederick Buttoni at the end of his six weeks' trial.' Bob Hirshin's voice echoed from the screen. 'Buttoni, found guilty of the mass murder of six student nurses, will spend the rest of his life in prison. Judge Stevenson added it would be a sorry day if Buttoni was ever allowed to be released, and recommended the six life sentences should run consecutively. Buttoni would face up to one hundred and twenty years in prison.' Bob reached for his glass of water. 'We'll be back after this short break with news from the war zone in East Africa, and how Senator Hewlitt suggests the US must be prepared for at least ten more years of fighting. This is Bob Hirshin for BCB News coming back to you after the commercial break.'

George stood and reached for the remote control to mute the volume. 'Ten more years of war; I don't know why they bother. The whole world seems to be fighting over something . . . .' he strode over to collect his toast, gratefully taking the plate from her. '. . . . what are they fighting about, anyway?'

'I don't know, George. I think some African country has managed to develop weapons that are a threat to another African country, and the Americans are sorting it out.' She sat back down at the table and looked longingly at her magazine. ' George . . . . do we really have to watch the news, it's so depressing?' but her plea was in vain.

'Yes, of course we have to watch the news. How else would we know what's going on? I suppose you would prefer . . . . soothing music from Radio Ga-ga.'

'Well, actually, yes, I would,' she put her glasses back on and frowning over them, picked up her magazine.

George ignored her and bit into his toast, pushed the volume button and gazed back towards the television.

'Welcome back to the world news, brought to you, live, from the BCB Newsdesk.' Again, Bob Hirshin's voice proudly emanated from the screen. 'Scientists have today issued a report claiming the use of stem cells to create human tissue is a giant step towards the replacement of degenerated organs and limbs. Dr. Kalowski, speaking for the Council for Human

Development, has also stated that it won't be too long before cells can be reproduced, and any decay of the human body will be replaced with life-giving material which will last for ever. This major breakthrough is thought to be the initial stages of 'everlasting life', although Dr. Kalowski commented there is still a long way to go before we can consider this new technique a reality for the future.'

'Hey, what about that? Soon we'll be able to live for ever.' George turned back to her, wiping the crumbs from his mouth.

'Yes, I suppose that's good . . . . but there's not much point in living for ever if you're going to be miserable!' Phoebe's curt reply was true in general, but George decided to take it as a personal attack. He folded his arms and defended himself.

'But Phoeb . . . . you know I'm just a little bit off it at the moment; I'm worried about money, and . . . . err, well I need to get some work . . . . you'll see . . . . after today I'll be better; more relaxed.' He was edgy now, thinking about the meeting.

Phoebe wasn't convinced, she had seen it all before. 'Yes, I know dear, but even when you were working, you didn't seem too happy, even then you still couldn't relax and enjoy life.'

Bob Hirshin smiled into the camera and took another drink of water. 'The Council for the State of Mental Health yesterday released its findings in a two hundred page report. The report, which has taken two years to produce, states quite categorically that the poor mental health situation across the western world is now at an all time high, with up to eighty-five percent of the population, at some point in their lives, using anti-depressants to combat the effects of stress.'

George walked slowly over to the television and switched it off, he could see Phoebe looking his way. He leaned over the granite worktop, staring vacantly out of the window towards the drizzly rain gusting through the now wasted flower beds which had looked so colourful in the summer. This was his chance, today he would prove himself . . . .

It was Phoebe who broke the silence. 'Anyway, it's ten forty-five, isn't it time you were getting ready?'

'Yes, err . . . . . maybe I should take my shower.'

'That's a good idea, darling.' She smiled graciously at him as he left *the kitchen and turned back to her magazine. At least now she could have a little peace . . . .*

. . . . With a jerk of his head, George suddenly opened his eyes again, his recollection of the morning's events vivid within his mind. It was unnatural to see these images so clearly and remember each conversation so distinctly, but this was exactly what he was doing. This was a strange place to be . . . . with a swift change of recall, he could step back in time with precise memory.

Standing up again, he opened the top button of his overcoat and walked tentatively over towards the books, reaching out his hand to touch the polished wooden shelving in front of him and instinctively pulled back as a glowing flash of green light raced across his hand and along his forearm. Feeling no pain, he reached out again, this time touching one of the elegantly-bound volumes. Again, the light jumped towards his fingertips, leaving an aura of violet mist swirling around his hand. He strained his eyes towards the immense chambers above his head, the light filtering softly down onto the Library floor. This wasn't a place he could possibly know.

George grimaced a little with the thought that maybe he *was* dead and this was the place where dead people lived . . . . but there was no-one else around. Perhaps they would send for him soon, when the time was right for him to meet with his maker. That's what the religious people said would happen . . . . after death you would be accountable for your sins . . . . they also said choirs of angels would greet you at the pearly gates . . . . but he hadn't heard any singing . . . . he decided it was just nonsense.

Positioning himself into a space between the rows of shelves, he allowed his vision to search for some form of hope, something he could recognise as life . . . . but his eyes told him he was alone. He called out in desperation. 'Hello, can anybody hear me?' but the vast echo of his words confirmed his fear. He would have to be patient and wait until something happened. It wouldn't be long, surely, until there was some form of contact made.

He walked helplessly back to the table, dropping into the chair, his confusion deepening with every breath . . . .

. . . . Yes . . . . *the blue suit, George decided, as he opened wide the wardrobe doors. Taking it out, he laid it neatly on the bed, removing a speck of dust from the collar. He reached under the bed and brought out his black brogue shoes and placed them next to his suit, returning back to the wardrobe for his best shirt. Sifting through the hangers, he soon realised it wasn't there. 'Phoeb, where's my shirt?' he shouted, hoping and praying she knew, but heard nothing.*

'Phoeb, my wedding and funeral shirt . . . . the white one . . . . where is it?' George was getting a bit flustered, but, as usual, Phoebe had the situation well under control, her calm voice drifted up the staircase.

'It's hanging in the airing cupboard, dear. I've washed and ironed it for you.'

'Oh . . . . right, thanks,' he uttered back in relief. 'I thought I'd wear my blue suit. What do you think?'

'Yes, dear.' Her patronising tone assured George his decision was good. He smiled to himself and rushed thankfully to the airing cupboard.

What was she to do with him? Sometimes he acted like an excited child. She shook her head and smiled ruefully, trying to focus yet again on her magazine, skipping through the pages with little conviction until her short interlude was interrupted.

'Right, I'm ready,' he called out, as he patted his briefcase, before making his way briskly down the stairs.

Phoebe glanced at the clock on the kitchen wall. 'It's eleven-twenty, dear. What time are you going?'

'Well, my train's at midday, so I ought to leave now . . . .' George answered, popping his head round the kitchen door, '. . . . to give myself time for a coffee at the shopping centre.'

She sprang from the table, pulling her dressing-gown snugly around her slight frame. 'Look, do you want me to drop you off, it's a bit miserable out there.' She nodded towards the heavy drizzle blowing threateningly onto the kitchen window. 'It's no trouble to get the car out.'

'No, I'll be fine, no need for you to bother . . . . the walk will do me good . . . . clear my head a bit.' They made eye contact and smiled. He loved the way she would always try to help. In any situation she was always ready to give of herself. Maybe he could learn a thing or two from her attitude.

'Well, if you're sure, but you had better put your overcoat on, it looks rough out there . . . . you don't want to arrive soaking wet!'

She joined him in the hallway as he lifted his coat from the peg and patted his trilby firmly to his head. 'Do you think I look smart enough?'

She tucked a clean handkerchief she'd taken out of the dresser drawer into his breast pocket. Men always neglected the finer details, but it was the little things that were important to her. 'Yes, you look fine, dear, I hope everything goes well.'

'Right . . . . well, I'm off. See you tonight.' He picked up his briefcase and moved towards her. 'Oh, and err . . . . happy anniversary.' He reached over and kissed her affectionately on the cheek. He could feel the love of ages rising in his heart as they touched.

'Yes, same to you, George.' Phoebe smiled and watched him step out through the front door. He was hard to please at times, but she couldn't help loving him.

George pulled his collar up tightly and set off for his walk down Wadsworth Road . . . .

. . . . The love of ages rested upon the stillness of the Library. Oh, how his love danced for Phoebe. How his heart beat rhythmically to the tune of their togetherness. How their song had risen beyond his thoughts, with an uplifting presence which settled all around this strange place.

He was close to her, but he couldn't touch her. He could feel her by his side, but he couldn't talk to her. He could cry out her name a thousand times . . . . but she couldn't hear his call. His frustrated yearnings were hopeless. He stared down at the table. This wasn't a dream. He nipped at his cheek in desperation. Come on . . . . come on . . . . wake up! But, he couldn't.

George exhaled his longings with a sigh as he pushed his elbows forward onto the table and dropped his head into his hands, whispering softly into the silence of the Library, 'What does it matter . . . . when I'm dead?'

'But you are not dead, George.'

The voice was soft and warm and seemed to come from everywhere, as if innumerable speakers had been strategically placed, so wherever you would choose to sit, you would be exactly in the centre . . . .

'Listen . . . . is that truth I hear,
to wash my doubt and cleanse my fear.'

'You see, George, you are not really who you think you are. You are not *only* the body that you so grandly use to strut about with upon the earth; energy is the truth behind the matter. Conscious energy of the universe is what you *truly* are, and, as the body will wither and decay, conscious energy can never be destroyed. It will live for ever and ever, for it is life itself.'

Again, the voice startled George. He jerked back and quickly scanned the room. He had expected some form of contact, but not like this. His heart raced a little faster knowing that now he may be able to find out what had happened to him, and the thought of this made him fear the worst.

He couldn't see anything or even guess the direction it was coming from. It was just there, everywhere, almost as if it were an echo coming from deep within, although he didn't understand a word it was saying. He listened, suspiciously gazing around the room.

'All your fears of death are a misguided belief that you are your *body*. A body that one day will be no more. Even your scientists, these days, would be in agreement that everything in the universe is made up of energy vibrating at different rates of frequency, creating its own magnetic field. They would also agree this energy cannot be destroyed. It can be changed into different form, at a new vibration . . . . but it cannot become non-existent. So you see, you can never die. For you are conscious energy, life everlasting. Death does not exist . . . .'

The voice was silent for a moment, leaving an air of suspense hanging all around the Library. George shuffled uneasily in his seat and was about to speak, when it continued.

' . . . . You and many other people have been living within the illusion that death, one day, will come knocking on your door. However, it is the *body* that no longer can serve its purpose. The life *within* the body, the consciousness, continues to live, and is released from the confines of its home of matter, returning to its true abode. A free spirit leaving the earth plane with the experience it has gathered. Does this answer your question, George?'

Again the silence. His adrenaline was racing as his eyes darted nervously in every direction. He couldn't remember asking a question at all and anyway, he didn't want to hear all this philosophical nonsense, he wanted to get out of here and go back to his life.

' I . . . . err, well . . . . err . . . . who are you?'

'Dear George, of course, I must have startled you. Let me introduce myself. I am the voice you have forgotten, the voice of reason, the voice of truth. Call me intuition if you so desire, for I am the voice of the heart, the voice of the universe, the voice that whispers softly in your ear to guide you through your darkest moments. I am the voice of love, the guardian of peace, the signpost to happiness. But, to put it simply . . . . I am you, George, I am your true self.'

Now he felt totally perplexed. He didn't seem to be getting anywhere and his patience was sinking fast. 'Look, if I'm not dead, what am I doing here? What is this place and can I go home now?' He raised his voice in frustration and his hands were physically shaking as he searched the room for an answer.

'There really is no need for you to go anywhere at the moment,' the voice remained calm and precise, 'everything you may want to know is here, in this Library. Everything that has ever happened and everything that will happen in the future is kept safe within these walls, locked into the knowledge of the universe. You are free here to look upon anything you desire, for you are sitting between 'no time' and 'all time'.'

George was beginning to think he was in some sort of madhouse. He wanted to physically see something, it wasn't easy talking to a voice that was making no sense and he wanted simple answers to his questions. 'I don't understand . . . . what do you mean?'

'I mean, wouldn't it be nice to be able to have a little chat for a while? You see, it seems such a long time since we have spoken to each other.'

Raising himself to his feet, he slowly stepped away from the table, towards the glowing shelves, peering around each corner in turn. 'But I don't know you . . . . I've not spoken to you before . . . . where are you? . . . . I want to see you.'

'Well, I'm afraid you will not be able to see me 'out there', you see, I am more of a friend from 'within' than someone you can see 'without'.'

George stood firm, still searching the vast area of books for signs of movement, he raised his vision higher scanning the ceilings for cameras, anything to fill in the questions of his mind. 'What are you doing here with me in this Library?'

'Well, I am always with you, constantly trying to communicate, but mostly my communication is without words. If you would listen to your heart, listen to your intuition, *then* you would hear the truth of my direction, for this is the way I would speak to you, through your feelings. You can only hear my words now because your little accident has brought us to a place where communication is easier for you to comprehend. But, it is usually through the silence, in the quiet of the mind, in the stillness of your heart, you will hear me.'

Now he had had enough and decided to try and think logically about the situation. He was getting nowhere with his questions . . . . the answers were making no sense at all. His instincts told him it must be a joke, set up by someone who was trying to ridicule him and would suddenly appear and shout 'got ya!' But that was crazy . . . . who would do such a thing? And anyway, the accident was real . . . . he wouldn't be here for any other reason . . . . and the voice was different, he certainly didn't recognise it as anyone he knew.

'What do you mean . . . . you're always with me?' He took a final glance into the brightly lit depths of the Library before tentatively returning to the security of the soft velvet chair.

'I am always with you, a part of you. Where do you think the ideas for the portfolio you have neatly put together for the job interview came from? Come on, George, wasn't that a bit inspired for you?'

George frowned and nervously fingered the buttons on his overcoat. 'How do you know about that? No-one could know about . . . . '

'The suggestion it was time to leave your job and work for yourself was my idea too . . . . let's turn the clock back thirty years or so to the New Year's Eve bash at the rugby club, it was me who gave you the notion to ask Phoebe to marry you. You see, sometimes you hear me . . . . but mostly you do not.'

'But why don't I hear you?' He cautiously stood up again and looked up and down the corridor, but could see no-one. 'Why don't I hear you all the time?'

'Let's just say you have been a little too busy doing other things.' The voice was very assuring with an easy manner.

George was puzzled and sat back down, folding his arms to defend his position, really now believing he was talking to a madman. 'What other things?'

'Things like living in an illusory world. Living within the confines of a world created by your thought patterns of conditioned responses and negative, fear based opinions. But to make it easy for you to comprehend, should we not just say you have been living the 'Story of George'.'

He decided to pacify the voice and go along with it for the moment, until he could work out what to do. 'But I am George, how else could I live?' He fidgeted uncomfortably, his thoughts racing, ' . . . . look, if this is some kind of joke, then let's get it over with, who are you and what do you want from me? I just want to get out of here.'

'You should calm down, George, and try to be patient and listen. I have told you I am your true self, and as such will help you with your life, if you will be so good as to give me your attention for a while. You will presently see that our conversation is no joking matter and that the confused state of your mind is nothing to be laughed at, although through the eyes of ignorance is constantly ignored.'

Suddenly he had a feeling from deep inside telling him this wasn't a joke, perhaps this was more serious and he *should* try to listen for a while, and, of course, he didn't want to appear ignorant. 'Yes, err . . . . but what are you trying to tell me?'

'What I am trying to tell you is that you are not really who you think you are. At the moment your mind is set into a false belief of who you are and of how you should interact with life. It is a story you have built up over many years, but let us turn the clock back and you may see that when you were born, there was no story of George. You were pure and innocent, as all babies are. It wasn't until you started to think that you began to create the false self that has troubled you all these years.

The conditioned responses to life, so innocently given to you by your parents and the cultural rules and belief systems of the place you were born into started to shape your thinking. The education system moulded your mind in preparation for what was expected of the young George as he reached maturity. Your likes and dislikes, the food you chose to eat, the habits you acquired, your needs and expectations of life were all gathered together and thrown into the mixing pot of *your* story, just like a jigsaw put together, piece after piece, bit by bit, until your desired creation took shape. All this, George, is an identity collected by you 'in time'. You have forgotten who you *truly* are, and have given yourself a false identity from which you cannot escape.'

The Library became still and silent as the voice stopped. Again, George didn't really understand, but the whole thing seemed to be about him and his way of life.

'Look, I'm a little bit confused about this. If I'm not dead . . . . I just want to go *back* to my life again. I have things to do that are important to me.'

'Yes, I know. Everything you do in life is important in some respect. But wouldn't it be nice to understand life a little better, so that you could apply good reason to it and feel that your purpose was coming from a much higher level? At the moment, you and many people on earth are living their lives at a very basic level, following cultural values and instinctive patterns which are leading you into a lifetime of discontent. Wouldn't it be satisfying to open up to a new and better way of looking at life, bringing a much more peaceful and loving world to live in?'

'Well . . . . yes . . . . I suppose so. Everybody wants a better world,' he raised his eyebrows, his thoughts falling onto the mixed up world he had come from, 'but how can *I* change it . . . . surely, it is, just as it is?'

'You can start by changing yourself. Take a look at the way you react and interact with life around you. It could be that, with a better understanding of 'who you are', you may start to see a new world rising.'

George blew out a deep breath and wiped his moist hands slowly over his hair, his thoughts still focused on escape, but at least he was listening.

'I want you to try and relax, you are still very edgy. There is nothing for you to worry about, everything will work out fine. Trust me, and know that all I say is for your own good.'

'Yes, yes, I'm trying hard to relax, but the whole thing is making me nervous. I can't understand why I'm here . . . . and my mind is telling me I must be dead. *You* have told me I'm not dead, but . . . . if I *am* alive, why am I here . . . . and why can't I go back?'

'Dear George, let me put your mind at rest. You are here because of the accident. It was a great shock to your physical and mental bodies, and has brought you to a different plane of consciousness As I have said before, it is a plane of no time, but all time. Now, because you are here, it is possible for you to look at the life you have left behind, and to question the way you were living it. Here it is possible to discuss many things with me, things that may help you to see life differently and hopefully allow you to return with a far greater perception of the truth.'

'So I can go back then?' The thought of this made him feel a little better but he was still suspicious. 'How do I know I can trust you . . . . ?'

'George, if you cannot trust yourself . . . . who can you trust? When we have finished our conversation, if your desires are to return to your life, then that is what you will do.'

At last, George could sense an end to his ordeal. He could go home! He closed his eyes, feeling relief washing over him, slowing his heartbeat to an easier rhythm. He relaxed deeper into the chair and tried to pull his thoughts together. What were his alternatives? The accident had brought him here, now he knew that much . . . . and he was alive with no sign of injury . . . . maybe he could trust the voice. What else could he do? Maybe he should just go along with the conversation and he would soon be home. After all, there didn't seem to be any other way he could leave this place. He decided to carry on, but he wasn't happy, he wasn't comfortable with any of this. He opened his eyes and unwillingly agreed. 'Let's get it over with then, what do you want to talk about?'

'Let us take a look at your life and see if we can unfold the story of George. Tell me a bit about your world.'

'Well, I, err . . . . what do you mean exactly?'

'I mean who are you? Tell me about yourself . . . . tell me about your life.'

George was quick to respond. 'Surely if you are who you say you are, then you already know all about me . . . . so what is the point of all this?'

'Yes, George, I am fully aware of who you are, this is not the problem . . . . it is *you* who I would prefer to understand yourself a little better, so if you would proceed, then we may take a step closer.'

He didn't want any of this, he wanted to skip the questions and just go home, but reluctantly started to speak out into the empty room with some embarrassment.

'Well . . . . I am George Eastwood, born in nineteen fifty-seven, the only child of John and Mary Eastwood, my parents . . . . I was educated at the local primary school and I, err, suppose you could say I was a bright child . . . . but I had to work hard to win a place at the local grammar school, where I sat examinations allowing me further education at one of the universities of Oxford . . . . there I studied business and media. After that I, err . . . . look, this is ridiculous . . . . how long do I have to carry on with this?' He felt uneasy and a little self-conscious about the whole thing and already his impatience had risen.

'That's good.' The voice ignored his question and carried on. 'And what did you learn from your parents, George? They must have been a big influence in your life.'

'Well, err . . . . my mother was very quiet and thoughtful, always with a good word for everybody. She was the one who really brought me up.' He was unnerved by the aroma of her perfume drifting once again into his nostrils and paused for a moment to steady himself. 'I remember my father seemed a little frightening to me in those days, maybe because I didn't see much of him, he was always at work, you see . . . . but my mother was always there to help me. The sad thing is, by the time I left for university, my father had passed away. He suffered a massive heart attack, killing him instantly and I never had the chance to really know him.' He felt a tinge of sadness remembering the death of his father and wondered why on earth he was telling the voice all this, but managed to compose himself and continue. 'My mother never managed to get over it, she was never the same, and she too, died a couple of years later of a brain tumour. Thank heavens by then I had met Phoebe. It was a hard time in my life, and Phoebe was wonderful, she helped me through it all, gave me strength to come to terms with it.' He reached out and picked up his hat, trying to reassure himself, delicately stroking the brim.

'All this must have been difficult for you, George, at such a young age . . . . but you managed to recover.'

'Yes, eventually . . . . Phoebe and I got married when I left university, and I managed to land a decent job as a journalist working for the local newspaper, and then progressed to assistant editor of a monthly periodical in Fleet Street. Those were happy days for me and Phoeb, and, of course, shortly after we started our family . . . .' he stopped momentarily, wondering when he would see them again, ' . . . . it all seems such a long time ago now . . . . and I suppose there are many things I could have done differently,' he added, having little desire to face any form of criticism from the voice.

'There are many things you *would* do differently now, George. Retrospectively, it is always easy to look at the choices you made and the changes you would make, but, at the time of occurrence, most people do the best they can.

Everyone is born into unique circumstances, allowing individual personality to develop. Everyone is born into a certain culture, with selected parents who pass on to the child firstly, a genetic code, forming the child physically, and secondly, a mental code of conduct that is set into the mind. I am sure that over the period of your early life it was quite common for people to comment that you were so much like your father or that you held many expressions of your mother.'

'Yes, it is true, but why is it so important?' he couldn't see the significance.

'I am only trying to make the point that there is nothing new about who you are; nothing you have discovered for yourself. Everything about you is second-hand information, mostly taken from your parents, education, nationalistic tradition and religion. Everything about you has been learned from other people and authoritative bodies which have told you the 'rights' and 'wrongs' of the society you were born into, all of which you have digested and followed blindly.'

George grimaced a little and really wanted to disagree. 'Well . . . . I'm not so sure about that. I have my own way of looking at things; my own ideas on how things should be done . . . . doesn't that make me individual?'

'Of course, but the mindset for your individuality has already been laid down by the society you were born into, consequently, it is difficult for you to think beyond those parameters. Take a good look at the world you come from, and tell me if you can see it running along smoothly. It doesn't take too much observation to see the violence erupting between countries and the aggressive tendencies of individuals towards each other. The centre of your attention has certainly become individual with a mindset which concentrates totally on the 'me' and chosen 'us', and is disrespectful to the rest of humanity. Is this who you are, George?'

Now he decided to argue. 'But we are proud to be different, we are proud to be born into our separate countries, with our own ways of living . . . . isn't that how it should be?' He dropped his hat back onto the table and stared down at it, pleased with his response.

'None of you are different at the core of your being, but systematically, authority has made you so. You are conditioned to believe that *your* nationality, *your* culture, *your* creed and *your* ideology are correct, and so you defend yourselves with the greatest of reason against the impostor which threatens your way of life. You may *say* you want 'peace', you may *say* 'we must stop this violence', which is so evident within your dissimilar societies, yet, there is a confused voice in the background which questions what can be done about it.'

Bob Hershin's voice echoed through George's head as he remembered the morning news. The world was in chaos, he could see that much, but still didn't understand why and certainly couldn't see what it was to do with him. He felt a responsibility for Phoebe and his kids . . . . but what could *he* do to change the world, what could *he* do to stop wars and violent behaviour. He shook his head in defiance, ' Well . . . . what *can* be done about it?' Surely it is up to the politicians and leaders of society to stop these things from happening?'

'It is a very serious question. Is there anything can be done at all? You are saying it is the leaders of the world, the presidents and governors, the ministers elected by the people who should stand up and speak with some form of resolution, some answer to your problem, but are they not human beings themselves, with the same prejudices and ideals as the rest of you? Are they not the same men and women who are buried into their own nationalism and tradition, into their own gods and selfish attitudes which divide the rest of society?'

George frowned, scratching his head, not wanting to give up on his argument. 'But these are intelligent people, if they can't find an answer . . . . who can?'

'Perhaps the answer will not come from intelligence, after all, through thousands of years of intellectual twisting and turning, trying to mould a new pattern of life, a new way which will satisfy the needs of every nation, colour and creed . . . . you are still here, looking for the same solution.

Intelligent thinking has brought with it vast technological breakthroughs, which no-one can deny has changed life beyond recognition. Scientists have made incredible discoveries about the earth and the universe; about the workings of the human species . . . . but has all this intelligent action actually changed anything? Has the intellect made possible a shift in thought which has broken down the barrier, allowing peace between nations, friendship and understanding between all men? Perhaps for all these years you have been looking in the wrong place to repair your broken world.'

George sat silently for a moment thinking about the voice's words. 'But I still don't see what it is I can do to help. I don't really understand about politics and all that stuff.'

'Perhaps you do not understand the ways of the political mind, George, but as I have said, maybe the problems of the world cannot be solved by political reasoning or intellectual change. Much more than this will be necessary to affect any form of reasonable change to a world that has become lost into its own deceit, much more will be needed to free the mind that has created such turmoil. If you can be patient, and listen carefully, then we may try to find an answer to the many problems man has to face in the world today.

The opportunity is here to look at the human problem with a more open mind; a mind that is free from reaction; free from the conditioning of thousands of years of past human behaviour. A new consciousness is necessary to bring about a radical change to the present culture and social structure, this much is obvious, but it is a change that starts by looking at yourself as an individual and *then* opening yourself up to the whole. This is what I want to talk to you about, here in this beautiful Library, where we will not be disturbed, where we may talk openly to each other and see if we can bring to light the truth of who you are.'

As the voice stopped, silence fell peacefully all around the Library, bringing stillness into the musky air. George sat quietly in disbelief, turning over the day's strange sequence of events. The accident; his arrival here; the voice he was hearing . . . . all seeming to be part of a plan to help him with his life . . . . but he didn't know why or how, he couldn't begin to understand the reasoning behind any of it. He didn't feel comfortable yet, and was still anxious about his future, still uncertain about the voice and the peculiar conversation they were having.

Folding his arms across his chest, he bit his bottom lip, not knowing quite what to think, he still wanted to leave this place and go home, and yet . . . . there was something inside him, tugging at his emotions, compelling him to listen . . . .

. . . . Phoebe Eastwood quietly closed the front door and let out an exasperated sigh. George had been hard work all morning, but she hadn't wanted to argue or upset him . . . . not on their anniversary. Walking quickly into the lounge to wave goodbye to him through the window, she peered round the curtain, but could already see him in the distance, head bowed, battling against the miserable weather. 'Bye, George,' she whispered softly to herself.

The weather hadn't been much better thirty years ago, on their wedding day. She distinctly remembered it was raining quite heavily in the morning but thankfully the heavy, dark clouds had given way to a much brighter sky by the time she arrived at the church. What a day it had been. A day to remember . . . . and she did, down to the smallest detail.

Her beautiful ivory dress, encrusted with pearls on the bodice and hem, still boxed and lovingly wrapped in tissue paper somewhere in the loft alongside the discarded children's toys . . . . and the deep turquoise bridesmaids' outfits her niece Debbie and best school friend Christine had worn. A wave of melancholy swept over her. How long had it been since she had seen either of them . . . . ? She felt again the slight rise of panic as she remembered the flowers and hairdresser arriving before she had barely had time for a cuppa . . . . she smiled with remembrance of her mother's oversized hat . . . . and the way her father lovingly squeezed her hand as they walked down the aisle.

Stepping into the kitchen to wash the breakfast dishes, she chuckled to herself as she fondly thought of George's facial expression as he turned to look at her walking towards him. What a picture. He was different then, with a naive innocence she had fallen for. A handsome young man with big ideas. She remembered the clumsy way he had said his wedding vows, as if he were being held at gunpoint, and then typically tripping over her hem as they proudly marched back through the congregation. Yes, it had certainly been a great day.

Taking out her pink rubber gloves from the drawer, she pulled them on, protecting her well-manicured hands as she squeezed lemon washing-up liquid onto the dishcloth and turned on the hot tap. Would she do it all again? She still loved him . . . . there was something special between them that couldn't be broken . . . . even though recently he was doing his best to annoy her with his constant grumblings. Maybe she should try to understand a little better. He was out of work and she knew it was bothering him more than he would admit. He was a proud man, brought up to be the bread-winner of the house and it wasn't doing his confidence any good struggling to find work, especially when it had been his decision to become self-employed . . . . it wasn't like George to make such a decision.

She recalled the first time she had told him of her pregnancy with Sonia. How excited he had been. How excited they both had been . . . . like young children finding the sweetie jar, and after all, they *were* young. She looked back with a longing to touch that giddy feeling of love and youth again. Was it the excitement of their new life together, setting up house and being pregnant, or was it the specialness of their love which had made everything seem so adventurous? They'd never had much money in those days, but somehow it had never seemed to bother them, being together was all that had mattered . . . . but, by the time she had given birth to Neville, it had all disappeared. It was as if a switch had been thrown to transform them into middle-aged people, more concerned about the cost of living than anything else. They still loved each other, without question, but nowadays, with the kids grown up, life had taken its toll and turned them into everything they swore they would never become.

It was funny how life could always make you feel there must be something more, something you were missing, but it wasn't that Phoebe was unhappy with life, she had everything that made her comfortable materially, it was just that she was frustrated . . . . she had a yearning now to feel more complete, although she didn't quite understand what was missing.

Some people may have said she had always had a very soft life with nothing to worry about, but that wasn't the truth. Yes, George had always made sure they had more than the basic needs, until recently, of course, but even then he had firmly refused her offer to find a job. He was a stubborn man with strong principals, and yet, she still felt the occasional pangs of guilt.

Anyway, she would have a nice cup of tea and then give Sonia a ring, just to see how things were going. Divorce could be such a messy affair and Sonia was certainly feeling the pain of it at the moment. It didn't happen too much in Phoebe's day; once the vows were taken, couples were expected to make a go of it, no matter what trials and tribulations were laid in their path.

She rinsed the dishes, shaking her head in despair and stacked them neatly on the draining board, removing her gloves and placing them back in the drawer before glancing up at the clock. Five to twelve. George would be well on his way by now. She prayed he would do well and get some work . . . . at least it might help him to settle down a bit and stop him feeling so anxious. His recent attitude had been too much to take, it was upsetting to see how disturbed and irritable he had become, but today, maybe he would take the first steps in recovering a little self-esteem and start to believe in himself again.

As she filled the kettle and switched it on, she hummed a little tune to herself, swaying her petite body to the beat. She felt lighter without George around, as if a weight had been lifted from her . . . . but of course, she would never tell him.

She dried a cup and saucer and waited patiently for the kettle, eventually pouring the boiling water on to the teabag, leaving it for a calculated two minutes before stirring it briskly and adding a minimum amount of milk. Even at her middle-aged years, Phoebe was still proud of her size ten figure, although allowed herself, as a special treat, a small digestive biscuit. She sighed as she completed her task and stepped airily towards the table with her drink and biscuit resting in her saucer. At last she could relax for a while, without interruption, without consideration for anybody but herself.

Momentarily her thoughts fell back to George, but she dismissed them quickly and reached for her glasses, eased herself onto the chair and continued to read her magazine . . . .

'And when it came to know the truth, I knew it straight away,
as if I'd always known it, but held it off at bay.'

'So . . . . . . where do we start, George? Where do we look to solve the problems of the human race? How is it possible that after thousands of years of human existence, of human thought and action, we could now take a look and speculate as to what is right or what is wrong?

Take a look around and you will see so many things which are not to your liking, so many questions unanswered, so many actions not to your approval, but it would be a task of unbelievable enormity to change each and every one of them. And then, even if it were possible, the change would not suit everybody, someone, somewhere, would cry out 'This is not what we want, this is not our way'. So where would we begin to assume a position where the slightest of change may be initiated?'

The voice was very assured and somehow made George feel important, as if anything was possible and he could be a part of it. He still felt disorientated in this curious place, still shocked by the events of his day, yet intrigued and wanted to hear more. 'Carry on . . . . I'm listening.' He spoke inquisitively into the calm.

'Let us be sure, then, what it is we are looking at. As we have said, it is not possible to lay down a set of rules and regulations which will fulfil the needs of all human beliefs, but it is possible to break down the barriers which have created such a separation, and to understand what is behind the problem.

I have suggested you are conditioned into a system of thought which allows you to operate, enables life to proceed - but in a confined, systematic way. You are allowed to think for yourself, build upon your separate ideals and moral code, and yet, your barriers have been fixed by nationalism, education, environment and parenting. Society has said to you 'this is how it will be', and sadly, you have followed. In short, life has become a very mechanical affair, mostly focusing on the 'me' which you have allowed to become the centre of your world.

I wonder what we would find if we were to strip away and remove the identity you have given yourself? To lift the barriers you have allowed to limit your thoughts and control your freedom would be a wonderful achievement. However, to do this we must take a closer look at the human mind and see if it is possible to understand the very basic operation of this complex mechanism.'

George wasn't sure he wanted this self-examination right now. He had never considered anything like this before . . . . why would he? . . . . he thought he was happy enough plodding along through the ups and downs of life. Maybe the voice *was* right, but after years of living a certain way, and then suddenly to question it, seemed a difficult thing to do, but he was listening, maybe slightly in awe of the voice and his surroundings, perhaps with a little disbelief for his predicament, but, nonetheless, he was listening.

'Have you ever been seated on a park bench, George, and watched a pigeon aimlessly wandering around pecking at this and that, endlessly following some form of driving force, some form of automated programming? After a while, you begin to realise the pigeon is not really having to think about life, in fact, it is living by very mechanical means - it is living by instinct. There is no problem for the pigeon to ponder over, there is no decision to take that would make it stop and think about what it is doing. Life for the pigeon is a constant cycle of eating, sleeping and procreating - the process of achievement is driven entirely by instinct.

If you were to examine any other of the beautiful groups of animals, either living in the wild or domestically cohabiting with humans, the same conclusions would be reached. Although other animals may not appear to be as basic as the pigeon, the same 'animal instincts' are predominant in their very nature, and upon closer inspection, you will see, George, these instinctive patterns of life are also found in the human species.'

'So we are no different from the animals?'

'For thousands of years man has shared this basic form of intelligence with plants and animals. All the work done by the instinctive mind is completed subconsciously, that is, you don't think too much about it, it is very much taken for granted. The work of repair, replacement, digestion, breathing, elimination of waste, etc., is being performed by this part of the mind. Every organ, cell and the purification and circulation of blood is supervised in this instinctive manner.'

'But I always believed it was the body that controlled all these functions.'

'The body has its own intelligence with which it carries out the necessary task, but initially it is brought into action by the instinctive part of the mind. The body actually does nothing of its own volition without the prompting messages from the mind. This is important for you to understand, George, the human body is an indescribable feat of nature's engineering, but is totally obedient to the mind which controls it.'

'Yes, err, right . . . . ' George didn't know why, but it seemed he had been drawn into the conversation by the very persuasive nature of the voice.

'If you would consider the fact that early man was little more than a basic animal, then you will understand that the instinctive qualities of the animal had to be predominant within man's nature. Life in the early stages was almost automatic, with a mental focus that was totally given to the physical side of life - satisfying primitive desires. He quite simply accepted his lot and asked no questions, for he did not recognise anything to question. Are you still with me, George?'

'Yes . . . . but I'm not sure why you are telling me about the human mind.' He had more important things to consider and didn't particularly want the science lesson.

'I am merely pointing out to you that the human mind has obviously progressed as it has evolved through the animal stages of development to the capabilities of modern man, but still has retained much of the instinctive ways found at the animal level.'

'But surely we are more than this . . . . the intelligence of man is far greater than that of the animals.'

'That is right. You see, as man started to evolve, so too, his mental attitude started to expand. This expansion of the mind brought with it a marked change that would differentiate man from the animal, a change that offered man the opportunity for major growth and the prospect of leaving behind some of the more unpleasant aspects of the animal kingdom. This transformation was the opening up of the second level of the mind, the intellect.'

George fidgeted in the chair, this reminded him of his schooldays, but the subject here was different to anything he could remember.

'So . . . . as the intellect started to unfold, it illuminated the instinctive ways of man with a new purpose - by adding reason to his life. It brought about a different mental approach, which in turn encouraged him to question what he was doing and why. Man began to look around and compare himself with others. He began to think for himself and analyse situations, passing on much improved data to his instinctive mind. It was the dawning of a new consciousness, a self-consciousness which has developed over the years and is now at the centre of modern man. The intellect has brought a new age; an age where man can make things happen for himself, without the confines of animal automation which kept him alongside the lower forms of life.'

'We have certainly come a long way.'

'Yes, man has developed an intelligence which has broadened his horizons way beyond instinctive response. Man now has a new focal point within, which allows him to take more notice of himself and the external world he has created. He is able to communicate, read books and store vast amounts of knowledge, obtain great wealth and accumulate material possessions. He can solve complex problems and change his environment with great technological breakthroughs, man can fly to the moon and sail the seven seas, filling his life with any pleasure he so desires . . . . and yet, he is so full of discontent.

It doesn't matter what he tries to fill his life with, there is still an emptiness, still a longing for more, still the desire to fulfil that which is always one step away. He may say to himself, 'If only I had 'this' or 'that', then I would be happy. If only I could be different, I would be at peace', but he is never satisfied, never content with his lot.'

Suddenly George became a little more alert. The subject had moved into an area he could relate to through his own experience of life. He sat forward now with better attention. 'But why does this happen?'

'As I have said, the big difference between man and the animal is an intelligence which enables man to think about who he is in relation to others. He has discovered a 'self' he may pamper, reshape and define into anything that he wishes himself to be - he can give himself credibility in a world which expects the best from everybody . . . . yet, he is fearful of the rejection which has become the indictment of his failure.

Man has become frightened, George. As his world progresses and he defines his own personal character, he also slowly starts to build up a legacy of fears; fears of an inner failure to fulfil his desires and fears of outer disaster striking his life. The human mind has become a strange mix of violence and peace, love and hate. It is both fearful and joyous, greedy and compassionate. One minute it is soft and gentle and the next it is angry and frustrated.'

George sat quietly with his arms folded, a puzzled look on his face. ' . . . . but this is who we are . . . . all the things you have mentioned, all the different emotions . . . . it is who we are, but we get on with it and do the best we can.' He was thinking of his own predicament.

'This is the way you have learned to cope with life and the many problems associated with it. The intellectual mind has brought many thoughts of an undesirable nature, many fears of bad things that could happen, but you are right, you have accepted this fact and buried your heads in the sand choosing to ignore the pain and get on with it.

But how is it possible that human beings who have lived on the earth for thousands of years, who are technologically so intelligent, have not been able to free themselves from such a problem? Moreover, it can be seen that as man expands his mental consciousness to greater levels of intelligence, so too does his fear multiply, making his mind extremely unstable.

If we look back in time to the early animal stages of evolution, we see that fear may have risen as a response to physical danger, but this was clearly an instinctive reaction to an immediate threat. Nowadays fear is an ever present pattern of thought which recycles a memory of pain and hurt into a preconceived future time or builds up a barrier of defence against the unknown. So we see that fear is not a legacy from the animal kingdom, fear is a state of mind brought about by the expansion of the intellect, it is a state of mind brought about by thought.'

'But we have to think, how else could we live our lives?'

'Thought is an inevitable consequence of the intellectual man, his belief is that without thought he could not better himself. Man believes himself to be measured by his intellectual prowess, and so the more he can think, the more power he believes he will retain. The intellectual centre, you may call it the ego or personality, through thought, has become separated from the rest of the world, and yet continually compares itself to images it sees in the outer world. It is a process which, over the years, has become such a great problem for man.

But let me explain, let me ask you this question: What do *you* think about the most?'

'Well, ... I'm not sure really . . . . '

'Yes, it is difficult for you to answer, perhaps because you don't even realise where your thoughts are. If you were truthful, you would see that your thoughts are predominantly about 'yourself', 'your life', 'your family', 'your job' . . . . the little world you have built for yourself and the prestige and power you have gathered into it. If you look closely, you will clearly see that most people think continually about the self, most people crave satisfaction and security for the identity they have made for themselves.'

George felt a little threatened now, as if his whole life was under the spotlight, but *he* was no different to anybody else, everybody was much the same. He shuffled around in the chair not knowing quite what to say.

'I . . . . I suppose that may be true.'

'My dear George, please relax, this is not a criticism. The human species is so full of beauty, but, should we not say that the true virtue of humanity has been lost somewhat? I am merely trying to point this out so that we can find a solution to your problems. If we can establish what is 'wrong', then perhaps we may see what is 'right'. Do not ever think my comments are of a personal nature, it is merely an observation for you to ponder over.'

He felt a little easier hearing this and tried to focus on the conversation again, but it was difficult to bring his full attention to something he didn't totally understand, and something he wasn't sure he wanted to understand. His thoughts drifted away towards his family, his life, the job interview he never made, the accident . . . . all flashing in and out of his mind . . . . and then he realised, the voice had got it right . . . . all he wanted to think about was himself.

'Over the years society has become so competitive in its nature that it is extremely difficult for individuals to think in any direction other than for the 'self'. It is a world where comparisons are constantly maintained between children as they grow and adults as they compete to be the best at what they do. Society has held up 'special people' with great achievements behind them or celebrities who have reached the height of power through commercial success as a benchmark for life's requirements.

Is it any wonder that the individual mind recognises material gain as strength and is constantly seeking for more and more, comparing its lowly position to that of others, and constantly hurting itself with fears of failure?'

This was exactly what George had been thinking about this morning, the awkward feeling of not being good enough. Why had he been so fearful of the job interview? He knew he was capable of doing the work . . . . but something inside told him that he may not be accepted, that he could be rejected . . . . now the voice was beginning to make sense.

'You see, most of you have accepted this way of life without questioning the truth of it. You have easily fallen into a highly competitive world believing it to be the only way of survival, in fact, many people appear to thrive on the ruthless realities of competition, lifting their profiles higher and higher, never ceasing to undermine anything of true importance, but it is doubtful that their minds may ever rest with a true peace and happiness, the like of which they continually search for.

Sometimes it is only when you question yourself, when you take a close look at your thoughts and attitude towards life, you may see just how mechanical life has become.'

George looked around sheepishly. 'You are right about society, it is so easy to be left behind if you haven't got the right mentality.'

'But this is just what I am saying, George, what is the right mentality? Man has evolved through the animal stage where his main concern was survival, his whole consciousness devoted to the physical side of life in a totally automated fashion, but the man of today has a new quest for survival, a mental challenge which puts him against a society that will never let him rest.

He is driven by a constant progression of thoughts, some of which have raised doubts and fears about his own self worth and credibility within the world he lives. He follows the latest trends and beliefs of a society that is forever changing, never able to accomplish anything of a permanent nature that can bring him peace of mind. He acts according to the ideals and traditions of the land he was born into and separates himself into his own little groups of similar belief. He spends his days wishing he had that special something which sets him above the rest, always seeking for that which will give him the security he so longs for, but it never comes and his mind and thoughts remain in turmoil.

Can you see this is happening in the world, George?'

After thinking about it for a few moments he nodded his head. 'Well . . . . yes, I can see what you are saying is true . . . . I suppose it's . . . . I mean, it does seem to happen that way . . . . but what can be done about it?' George began to feel a surge of curiosity racing through his mind, his own life seemed to be a persistent struggle, and he wanted to put it right if it was possible.

'For most of you the difficulty lies in not being free from the old habits of thought. If you were to try and look at the movement of life as one thing, not as an Englishman or European, Christian or Muslim with personal tradition and culture, but as a free spirit without attachment to ideals and conditions, immediately your world would become a better place.

Just to pause for a moment and give attention to your mind is enough to raise the energies of a new consciousness, a new awareness within. This is what I want to tell you, this is where your solution lies - in knowing who you truly are.'

'So there *is* something we can do?'

'First of all the solution will come from actually seeing there is a problem in the first place. Many people are happy to follow blindly what they have become used to, but there is a part of you which is not filled with the conflict of thought, there is a part of you which questions the confusion that has become your world. It is a place where there is no judgement or condemnation, but is alive with trust, honesty, generosity and every possible virtue which wakes up the 'better' side of man. It is the higher level of the mind where there is such awareness to raise the consciousness of man. This place we will call the spiritual mind.'

George's thoughts flashed immediately to Phoebe, the book she had tried to persuade him to read and his cynical reaction. It was strange now, sitting here in this surreal place, discussing matters that Phoebe would just love to be a part of. Strange indeed, that it was him listening to a conversation that yesterday he would have laughed at, but now he didn't feel like laughing.

'Now, the spiritual mind does not work contrary to the intellect - it simply goes beyond intellect and passes down certain truths, then leaves the intellect to digest and reason with them. Spiritual consciousness is warm and alive with higher feelings and allows the intellect to promote kind and loving thoughts towards his fellow man. He feels impulses reaching him from a place unknown, a place within, which allows him to empathise with compassion for the world, something that was not possible through his instinctive nature. It hurts him to see others suffering, and when it hurts him enough, he tries to do something about it.

As time goes by, and he feels this pain more and more, it will be impossible for man to suffer, because man will not allow it. The pain of it will be too great and he will insist that its source must be changed.

The spiritual mind is also the source of divine creation, the place where poets and painters, songwriters and orators take their inspiration to impress the world with their great visions and foresight. It is the place where certain spiritual powers are made available to those who can progress beyond the attraction of the lower nature, a place of peace and harmony which will extend itself to the whole of the human race, as and when man decides to listen to its words of freedom. He has long since forgotten that everything he could wish for already lies silently within himself.'

'So all of this is inside me now, waiting to show itself?'

'It is certainly there, George, and even though you may not be too aware of it, the finer energies of the spiritual mind are constantly flowing into your emotions. Many times your compassion has risen when you have seen something happen in the world that your heart will not accept. Many times you have questioned yourself as to the truth you are following and consequently opened your mind to messages of a higher nature. Everybody has opportunity to listen, to feel the truth of any situation, but sometimes you are lost into your other world of thought, and so you do not hear.'

'So . . . . so . . . . it is your voice I am listening to . . . . through the spiritual mind . . . . that is where you are?'

'If for one moment you can escape the endless thought patterns of the 'self', you will feel a presence rising in your heart. It will be a feeling of contentment and joy, a feeling of inner peace and love. The presence you feel will be me, George, or should I say, it will be the true self that you are.'

The Library fell into silence again as the voice ceased. George folded his arms and filled his lungs with the deepest of breaths, slowly trying to comprehend the conversation.

He could understand the basic evolution of man from the animal stages to an intellectual development of the mind and he could see that this new consciousness of thought had brought with it many problems. Man had great intelligence now to do things which made life much easier in many ways, but life had become complicated, full of rules and regulations, moral codes and justifications, it was all too much to take in.

The voice was right, society was cruel, dishonest and judgemental . . . . it was difficult to trust anybody when there was so much greed for material gain and so much pressure to do better than anyone else. It was all too stressful for him now, too demanding at his age.

He was frightened of life, frightened of what life could throw at him, worried about his health, worried about money, even concerned about his family and his relationship with Phoebe. He was a mess, under pressure to make his life work . . . . but why did he feel under pressure?

He loved his family, all he had ever wanted was to be happy together, without all the arguments. He wanted something more for them, he wanted to find a 'better self' . . . . whatever the voice was talking about . . . . he wanted to find it.

'You see, George, this is what I want you to question, this is what I want you to focus your attention on and to decide which part of you is real and which part of you is not.

Man has created for himself many images of how he should be, how he should react and interact with his outer world. He has produced many facets to make himself accountable for his actions in a society which has become, to say the least, unstable and unsure of the way forward . . . . but where does the truth of man hide?

There is a 'false self' which asserts meaningless pressure onto such a mind that has become dull and follows blindly the beliefs and ideals of its own little world, desperately seeking to find some form of security and yet falling more and more into a state of confusion. Is this the reality of the world you live in, George . . . . have you forgotten the truth of who you are?' . . . .

LIVE IN PEACE

'And a child did ask the question,
"Why do you fight, when peace is written in your heart?"
. . . . . . and a great silence fell about.'

George raised himself slowly to his feet, sluggishly pulling at the buttons on his overcoat until each one was opened. He slipped out of it and laid it neatly on the table in front of him, alongside his hat. He loosened his tie, and then with a jolt, remembered his mobile phone in the pocket. His heart beat a little faster as he quickly bent over and lifted it out . . . . but it was dead. He despondently placed it on the table and sat back down, pulling his chair closer. He leaned forward, drumming his fingers onto the beautifully grained pattern, first his left hand, then his right, beating out a rhythm that echoed through the silence.

What else did he expect? What did he hope to find in this weird and surreal place? He slid the phone back into his pocket, pushing his briefcase firmly under the table away from his feet. What a day it had been. He had left home full of anticipation for a successful meeting, but in his wildest of dreams could never have envisaged he would be sitting here in this mystical Library, holding a deep conversation with a voice claiming to be him.

He exhaled with a sigh of submission, smoothing back his hair in his habitual way and shuffled back down into the soft velvet upholstery, still believing that the easiest way to get back home was to just go along with the voice. Anyway, it had been quite interesting listening to what it had to say . . . . and maybe there was some truth to it. At least it had made him sit up and listen, something he didn't believe possible when he had first arrived here. It had certainly made him think about the state of his own mind and the mad society he was living in.

The voice was right, everybody seemed to be disconnected, cut off from each other, each one lost into his own little world, separated by his own thoughts of how life should be. There was no communication any more, nobody had time to stop and talk, chat about the things that really mattered, everything was moving at such a pace . . . . it was difficult to keep up.

His thoughts continued searching his mind for answers: Why was this happening to him? What was it all about? . . . . but then fell upon a lighter place as they shifted to Phoebe. His heart fluttered a little, giving rise to a gentle sigh which whispered softly into the peaceful environment. What would she think if she could see him now? What would she say to him if he could speak to her, tell her of the Library and the voice? If only she knew about the accident . . . . again he remembered . . . . the wind and the rain and the car heading menacingly towards him. It was clear in his mind, and yet, for some reason, felt like a memory from a long time ago. Like a visit to the dentist, he could remember feeling the pain, but he couldn't recall what the pain was like. He grimaced a little and looked at his watch: five to twelve, it had stopped exactly at the time of the accident.

Gently rubbing his eyes he wondered what would happen to him now. How long would it be before he could go home? He was still anxious about his future, but he would try to be patient and listen, after all, he was becoming intrigued with the conversation, and it couldn't do him any harm. He trusted the voice, but didn't know why. There was something about it that made him believe, something that held him captive and reeled him in. He felt a comfort from it, like an arm of compassion around his shoulder or a word of kindness after a fall.

George sat patiently in the silence and waited, glancing down the long corridor, following his vision to a point where everything he could see merged into a single light, a point that danced before him, holding his attention firmly within a mist of white and green vapour, rising and falling around a halo of candle light. His eyes widened and fell upon the glow of magical colour inviting him from his chair, mesmerising his being with a desire to touch its faultless beauty. He stood up and walked on, down past the tables and chairs, beyond the rows and rows of books, gliding his body towards a myriad of lights glistening above the candle flame. He strode closer, closer to the light that beckoned his arrival as if it had waited forever for this moment, just to open its secret and touch his hand gently to guide him along. He breathed deeply into the midst of its enigmatic colour.

What was that smell? His senses told him gunpowder and cordite, a smell he didn't understand, and yet recognition seemed to rise up from within like an instinct of retrieval emerging from a place he didn't know. Suddenly, he could hear the shells rising and then falling into a deafening explosion, screeching into the silence, shaking the floor of the great Library. He halted his approach and stood firm. He could hear the shouts of men, as if scurrying to safety through the aftermath of bombardment and frightened cries of horses against the merciless explosions of unrest, the rat-tat-tat of gun fire and the groans of despair crying out for help. He could smell the stench of a world fallen into the fires of hell, the drifting touch of fear swelling in his nostrils and reaching deep, deep into his torso like a river of pain that rooted his feet to the floor.

Breathing heavily into the vast mist of despair, his eyes fixed closely on the candle, he moved slowly forward again, reaching out to its guiding light . . . . and then it was no more . . . . the smell had risen, the battlefield silenced and the mist vanished, disappeared into the heavens of the Library . . . . and again the silence.

George paused, gazing at the candlelight, his eyes transfixed to a small area of bright light opening up in front of him with a magnificence of intensity. He could feel his heart, racing faster and pounding with a pulsating beat within his chest. What was happening to him now? His senses were sharpened, pulling him closer and closer to the light. He stepped forward to stand within its glow, feeling the brilliance of its touch surrounding him with a warmth that lifted him gently towards its centre. Suddenly he stopped again, his eyes widening, as he glanced down towards the vision set before him.

Now he could clearly see him. The soldier in his shoddy uniform, scorched at the elbows, muddy on the knees, sitting mindfully at a small table with pen and paper, writing his thoughts, so to be remembered.

George looked closely at his new vision tunnelled deep inside the yellow clay: the corrugated metal roof sheltering the frail image; the small wooden table with candle lighting the paper; the photograph of a young female placed at one end, smartly dressed and smiling with studio pose; the sandbags seating him close to his writing and unforgotten love. He was a young man, not more than nineteen or twenty, with half-shaven head and piercing eyes that spoke beyond his years. His torso was thin, too small for the khaki uniform that hung from his shoulders and folded heavily around his midriff as he fell forward to his writing.

George called out. 'Hello! You down there, hello.' But there was no reply, just the sound of pen scratching upon paper. He tried again. 'Can you hear me? Hello.' He stepped forward towards the soldier, but couldn't raise response to his words. He glanced down towards the table and allowed his eyes to reach beyond the dim candlelight to read the soldier's word . . . .

The trench was long and deep.
Long to a point beyond vision,
turning at its furthest point to become infinite through human eyes.
Deep to a depth that swallowed and devoured
the tallest of our human frame,
and sheltered gladly, as a wall of mother's love
protecting our fears and blessing our dreams with a caress of safety.

Along its length sat groups of men, huddled around each other,
with talk of words which spoke of days gone by
and dreams left waiting to fulfil.
Hearts of love, songs of unsatisfied desire which lived beyond this place,
beyond this no-man's-land of deserted promises.

But yet,
promises of return echoed through the words of hope and confused belief,
lingering like a mist of time,
waiting to be heard again.

A haze of smoke lifted and fell openly like a cloud of paradise
and lingered beyond the sand bags and helmets,
whispering softly and rising where no man would lift himself
with ease of comfort.

And silence,
as the sun fell beyond the fringes of hell,
to raise the blood coloured sky as curtain to our theatre of pain.
A moment of peace, when hearts did forget,
a moment of hope,
when hearts did leave this place with safe return to love,
waving its desire with the beauty of our remembrance.

Oh Father of this hell,
this cannot be what you would choose for your son.
This cannot live but to tell a world that despair
and dreams of war are nothing
but a fever upon our peaceful nature.

We are souls of tragedy,
spirits of hell, walking bravely along our corridor of fear,
huddled in our trench of safety,
where honesty has returned to our hearts
like a whisper of our greatest truth ....

And we gathered there, speechless,
rendered silent behind our heavy breath,
transfixed with uncertain sounds from beyond this wall of destiny.

A glance of hope,
to take its strength from brothers in arms,
waiting for tomorrow's wisdom
to bless our march for freedom.

And we waited for a moment ....

And a whistle of time did tell us
tomorrow was here.

. . . .The soldier laid down his pen and lovingly touched the photograph of the young woman. He picked it up and held it closely to him for a moment, his eyes glistening in the light of the candle, searching for a love that was far away. Slowly he removed his writing from the table and carefully wrapped it around the photograph, placing both of them, out of sight, in the inside pocket of his soiled uniform. He pulled out a half-smoked cigarette and struck a match on the rough surface of the table top. Inhaling deeply, he gazed around his makeshift shelter, blowing a stream of swirling smoke into the still, dark air. He stared hopelessly into the crumbling, yellow clay, where revengeful attack had shaken its solidity. His eyes closed for a moment as he savoured another intake of smoke, quickly exhaling and spitting out the loose tobacco. Reaching round, he lifted a tin helmet from the floor and pushed it tightly to his head, grasping, as he did, for the butt of his rifle leaning restfully against the wall. He took a last draw on the tiny stub and crushed it under his muddy boot.

George watched with eyes wide and mouth open, as the soldier raised himself from the table, blowing out the candle with a swift burst of smoky breath. And as the mist returned, swirling silently around the oaken floor of the Library, the soldier's world was gone . . . . gone to the mists of time.

George stepped back, away from the returning mist, his eyes scouring the room for the soldier's image so boldly planted into his memory. But it was lost now, lost into another world, lost into the vastness of this great Library. He stumbled backwards onto the floor, still searching every direction, but to no avail, it was over. He noticed his hands were shaking, his breathing quick and heavy with the surge of emotion, driving his heartbeat to the rhythm of a drum. He tried to pull himself together by breathing more slowly and deeply, hoping to relax and release his disturbing images.

'Are you alright, George . . . . is there anything I can do to help?' The voice broke the silence with an air of compassion.

George was startled, quickly darting his eyes around the room. 'Oh . . . . well, I err . . . . just feel a little strange.' He was still shaking. 'You see, I err . . . . just had the weirdest experience.'

'Yes, I know, I was with you through it all, but there is nothing for you to be afraid of.'

He felt less alone as the comforting voice settled his being.

'But that was the strangest thing I've ever encountered. I was there . . . . right in the middle of the soldier's world, but . . . . but he couldn't see me, he couldn't hear my words, and yet . . . . it was so real . . . . as if I was living it myself.'

'Let me explain what has happened. You see, George, your memory has taken you into another time and place where you were able to witness a great evolutionary step being made. A time when many young souls, through terrible physical and emotional persecution, came to know the insanity of war and question why it should be.'

'You mean the first world war?' His reply was purely instinctive.

'Yes, we *are* talking about that period in history, but more to the point, we are looking at a certain time within that treacherous offensive. The images you have looked upon, the emotional pain you have felt, was precisely a certain night within that cold hostility. It was June the thirtieth, nineteen-sixteen . . . . the eve of the bloodiest battle. You have looked upon the last moments of a young soldier's life, torn apart by the ravages of war, leaving him in desperation, hopeless despair, and certain knowledge this was not how it should be, his final thoughts written down for posterity with a plea to stop this terrible conflict. He could see, as many others were to know, the hypocrisy of war should be released for ever.'

'But why did I need to see that? Why did I have to see those images?'

'Because as the young soldier marched out of his trench, towards his certain death, he took with him a very important part of the universe . . . . you see, George . . . . the soldier was you.'

A silence hung around the Library as George tried to take in the voice's bold statement, he felt the blood drain from his face. 'What do you mean . . . . the soldier was me?' He clasped his hands together, squeezing them tightly, trying to make sense of it all.

'Just take it easy, I know all this will come as a shock to you, I say again, there is nothing for you to worry about . . . . all of this, is indeed in the past, another lifetime of experience. Even then, you were a writer, trying to make clear the madness of war. Your name was John Taylor, a soldier of the British Fourth Army, destined to fight and lose his life on the very first offensive of the bloodiest battle the world has ever seen. Tens of thousands of men were taken in the first days of that tragic encounter.'

At last, he blurted out his thoughts. 'But this is incredible . . . . you mean it was me? You are saying I have just watched *myself* all those years ago? . . . . Surely that's not possible?'

'The truth is, you have lived many lifetimes, each with its own evolutionary purpose, bringing you closer to the truth of who you are. But for now, it is enough for us to consider your experience of war. This was a difficult time, but served your evolution well and has made you the peaceful man you are today.'

George put his head into his hands. His eyes welled with tears, touched by an unbelievable sadness and compassion he had not felt before. He had seen plenty of images on TV about the war and had never been able to understand why it should happen . . . . but for him to be a part of it was too much to take in. He took the clean handkerchief Phoebe had given him out of his pocket and wiped away at his face, breathing deeply to calm his emotions.

'Dear George, let me try to make some sense out of your distress. It does not take too much thought to know that over the ages man has fought his wars again and again. In whatever circumstances, with any and every means at his disposal, he has continually battled, nation against nation, man against man, without regard for the consequences of his action, without respect for loss of life. In the most barbaric to the highest, most sophisticated ways, man has aggressively fought for his cause. He has won and he has lost. He has lived through it, and he has died because of it. The great question is *why?*'

Feeling a wave of empathy from the voice, George felt more comfortable and slowly arched his back, pushing his handkerchief away into his trouser pocket.

'Now, we could try and answer the question by defending man and claiming he has no choice but to fight, that it is an instinct set deep into his psyche. The instinctive mind is primed with a deep rooted sense of fighting instinct which has served man well over many, many years, and has been called upon quite successfully when danger has risen to threaten his existence. But this is a momentary decision of the mind in a situation that has called for instinctive action. When life is threatened in any such way, it can be seen immediately that the 'animal response' is sure to kick in with a 'fight or flight' answer to counteract the danger perceived.

But, if we look closer at man, we will quite clearly see that war is not an instinct. War is a pre-meditated state of imbalance, which totally opposes his true, peaceful nature. Wars are prepared for, with great tactical plans; armies put together, trained for action; armaments set and pointed to the skies. Airways are patrolled constantly with radar and fighter jet; seas and ports guarded against external attack; politicians concerned over offensive actions taking place thousands of miles away - war is ready to be used, ready and waiting to take its action.'

George knew this was true, every country had its own army and defence system, every country was ready to spring into action at the slightest sight of trouble. He had never been able to understand it, but all over the world wars were still going on . . . . and he didn't know why this was happening in the twenty-first century. 'But . . . . nobody wants to fight, nobody wants to see countries at war with each other . . . . this is the ridiculous thing about it . . . . everybody wants to live in peace.' He spoke out with quite a passion burning in his words.

'Then why do you fight at all, George, why do you bother if it is peace you want?'

This was a difficult question. He knew sometimes a country had to fight in order to bring about peace. The politicians did everything they could, but if there was too great a threat, then something positive had to be done to eliminate the danger.

'Well . . . . I, err . . . . suppose we have to . . . . sometimes we are threatened by other countries and . . . . we have to defend ourselves.' He stuttered out his reply with little conviction.

'So your answer to this delicate question is that you do want peace but, in the event of something or somebody threatening your way of life . . . . you will violently defend your position.'

George realised it did sound a bit odd, but it was true, what else could be done? 'You make it sound as if it is wrong . . . . surely it is right to do this.'

'You see, George, society has developed a strange morality; you say that peace is the way, everybody wants peace, and yet you are quite willing to kill and mame when your peace is disturbed. Society has decided that it is acceptable to kill others in the name of country, in the name of God, or in the name of some other collective belief, but to kill within your own community is considered totally unacceptable - such morality is strange indeed.'

'Well we can't just go about killing each other . . . . it would be wrong to do that.'

'Then what is it that makes man send his war machine into action? If you say it is wrong to go about killing each other, then it must be something of vast importance which makes you do so - it must be something that intelligence cannot comprehend which makes you do 'wrong' in the belief it is 'right'. What could it possibly be that can turn you away from the greatest principles you hold and persuade you that violent attack is the answer?'

'Well, err . . . . as I say, sometimes we have to fight.' He was starting to feel a little embarrassed now but had decided to stick to his principles.

'Could it be fear that drives you towards such extreme actions? Could it be something inside your mind that twists and turns your thoughts into such a state of panic that your reaction is to strike out before it is too late?

You see, man lives within boundaries of national identity and has given himself cultural and political ideologies, rules and regulations to live by. He has pledged himself to his own personal religious belief and has developed a tradition he believes to be the right and proper way of living. All this he has done in the belief it will give him security and bring him the peace he is looking for, all this is an identity he has collected which makes him feel safe in a world of separate systems of belief. But it is when this identity, this security, is threatened, do we see violence erupt in man.'

'But these are the differences between nations, this is where the trouble begins.'

'You have said it, George, this is where the trouble begins, but the differences between man only come from a dissimilar conditioned state of mind. There is no truth in the assessment of one man being different from another. It is all part of a grand illusion he has created for himself, nevertheless, it is an illusion that he sees as a threat to his wellbeing.

It is this morality of judgement with which man builds his world of self-preservation. He attempts to build up a secure way of life for himself and then protects it against any perceived intrusion . . . . whether it be real or not. He not only lives in fear of losing 'his house', 'his car', 'his job' and 'his money', but moreover, from a collective point of view, fears his whole way of life may be threatened as in 'his nationality', 'his tradition' or 'his religion' and a new order imposed upon his weakened state of mind . . . . and so he builds his world and places a fortress around everything he has called 'mine'. He protects at all costs everything which makes him feel secure. But even then, his fear of loss will never allow him peace of mind, hence he lives in a permanent state of imbalance - a cycle of security, fear and violence. This is the madness of man.

The world you have created is turning in a state of conflict which makes attack seem reasonable and honestly provoked. It has given rise to a defensiveness which makes peace impossible to achieve, and it is when whole nations fall into this belief that war is inevitable.'

George shuffled around on the hard wooden floor, staring intently back towards the location of his vision, where the last wisps of mist were now floating gently upwards into the vast chamber. He knew war was a terrible thing, but it did happen.

He questioned the voice. 'But why is it such a bad thing to try and defend ourselves?'

'Defensiveness stems from fear. Fear that everything you hold dear will be attacked and taken away from you. Look at the structure of the world, look at all the defence mechanisms you have put in place for your protection. All your legal definitions and penal sentences, your insurance policies and all your heavy armaments serve only to preserve its sense of threat. It is as if a wall of fear has been built around you tightening its grip with each device you use to strengthen its defence. It is imprisonment of the mind in the most insane way.'

'But there are people out there who will attack us. There are countries and organisations that threaten our way of life . . . . surely we must protect our society?' Suddenly, he realised that now he was condoning the actions of war.

'Then maybe you need to ask the question: 'What am I defending myself against?', for in truth, you will find that your aggressors are living within the same confusion that has twisted your own thinking. You will find that their own attack is a statement of the same fear which has clouded your world. This is the hypocrisy of defensiveness, it is an illusion of the mind, but unfortunately, it is an illusion you have come to believe in. Defences are the costliest of all insane beliefs created by the intellect. They are a never-ending barrage of self-abuse, and grow stronger the more you tighten your locks and build up your armaments.

You see, if the intellect is left to its own devices it will seek out whatever means it can to ensure its survival. It will turn its attention to the protection of everything it has created and will build a defence system which it believes will give it strength and power over anything that would threaten its safety.

This naive thought process may be seen all over the world as countries jostle with each other, claiming to hold the greater power of world domination as they build up vast defences of armaments. Allies are taken to strengthen these defences which enable more power to be thrust upon the smaller nations, who have little defence against it.'

George's mind flashed back to the news, only this morning he had been watching a clear example of this peculiar policing of smaller African states.

'It is a world of 'playground bullying' as the stronger nations yield a sword of fear against what they perceive as threat from different cultures and religious beliefs, allowing fear to rise in their hearts before trying to understand that these differences are not a threat to their wellbeing. It is a world without trust, a world that is mistaken in its belief that external power is strength. This is not who you are, George. It is a sad reflection of a society forced to live with a constant fear of attack.

All your defence systems have been built ultimately to protect your fears. When you can understand this, then you will know that what you defend against are just mad illusions of the mind. Slowly at first, you can let go of your defences, but confidence will grow as your trust increases. With this trust it is not danger that comes when defences are laid down, it is safety, it is happiness and it is peace.'

He was beginning to see the validity of the voice's word, it would be a much better world to live in if all defences were laid down. He couldn't see the point of having weapons of mass destruction when the thought of such devastation brought about the greatest of fear. It surely had to be the way forward to release the tensions between countries and, as the voice had said, a trust could be built up again. From his point of view it had to be worth a try.

'Yes, surely it would be better to talk about these things than to attack without good reason.'

'But this is the problem, everybody believes they *have* good reason. It is a legacy of your separated mental state which tells you it is justifiably correct to attack each other. You may think there is great value in the fact that you are British, Chinese, Indian or American, but when you look closely, you will see that nationality actually breeds wars. You may be proud to stand tall for a Christian, Muslim or Jewish system of belief, but when pride incites violence and aggression your outer world cannot be at peace.

While ever man is caught up into such ideals of separated expression it is impossible for him to reach a verbal arrangement which brings unity and peace to all parties. No matter how long he sits and talks of alliances and peace treaties, his mental consciousness will still form a conflict of opinion. By all means talk, but if it is peace you seek, then talk of peace and don't let your petty little differences interfere.

Allow the intellect to hear the impulses of the spiritual mind. This will be an honest appraisal of the situation, giving rise to a kinder, more caring attitude, showing concern and compassion for all parties involved. Decisions will be made through a higher consciousness, with the interest of world peace at heart, and not the grim despair of war. You are not basic animals any more, so why do you act as such?

If you were to sit back and carefully think about what you do, you would realise that to attack will only reinforce the strength of your fear. You actually make stronger what you defend against, until it becomes inescapable. This is a universal truth. All of your wars are based around the insane belief that you can protect your fears by attack. It is a cycle of unrest that can never be broken until you allow defencelessness to rise out of your true self.'

Again, listening to the voice, George's thoughts had become much more positive. Now he could at least see a solution to the impossible question of war, a problem which never seemed to go away.

He pushed firmly with his hands against the floor, raising himself to his knees and gradually straightened up, stretching his arms and bending his back to release the stiffness from his limbs. He thought about what he had seen. Himself as a soldier, so earnestly fighting for peace, a vision of hopelessness before his eyes. He thought of the world he lived in now, with all its systems of protection, all its codes and ethics and promises of a better future, which never came to fruition. He thought about the voice's words, strong and passionate with a desire to help. Were they truthful? Was it possible that defences created a world of unrest? His heart told him the voice was speaking the truth.

He walked thoughtfully back down the corridor of the great Library, back down past the books, back to the tables and chairs that welcomed him with a warm glow of light. Seating himself back in the soft velvet chair, he gazed reflectively down at the table, his overcoat resting across the grained pattern of its rosewood surface. A feeling of melancholy filtered through his emotions leaving him with a sadness for the plight of the human race. It was puzzling for him to see so clearly the confused state of the human mind, only this morning he had been living in the middle of it, but now he was beginning to step back a little and see where the problems were coming from, at least.

'Do you know something, voice . . . . I'm beginning to like you.'
'You have no reason not to, George, only your fear of the truth' . . . .

*'How still upon a silent world does peace rest easily,
with not a cry and not a shout, is all that peace would be,
but like a whisper rested there, upon a silent prayer,
for all who know the ways of peace, would know when it's not there.'*

Phoebe Eastwood finished her tea and put her cup down on the table. She felt restless. A knot of anxiety twisted around her solar plexus making her toss her magazine down in frustration. Maybe George had left her with his anxiety, he hadn't been at his best, and she felt sure she had picked it up from him. She shook her head and smiled as she imagined a germ of uneasiness attacking her from another person . . . . but she knew it was just her sensitivity telling her something wasn't right.

Phoebe liked to think she was intuitive enough to be able to sense when things were wrong with someone else, but she hadn't quite learned how to resist taking it on herself. She should let it go . . . . George was George. If he wanted to be anxious, then so be it. It was his decision.

She gave up on her magazine and picked up the newspaper, flicking through it, looking for something interesting to read. Page after page of celebrity gossip; political speak; economic disaster; tragic tales of human lives with photography for impact. She tried to read bits here and bits there, but couldn't find much interest in any of it. Sonia was on her mind.

Phoebe, like most mothers, was having great difficulty letting go of her children, even though they were grown now, she felt a responsibility for their happiness. She had watched them wandering through life, making the same mistakes she had made, but when she had tried to tell them, or offer good advice, it had not been appreciated. The best way, she had decided, was to let them find out for themselves. As George always said, at least afterwards you can say 'I told you so.' But for her, there was no pleasure in this *or* watching them make mistakes. She would be there to help them, if they needed it, but she *would* try and keep her nose out and let them get on with it.

She sighed, and closed the newspaper. Perhaps she would give Sonia a call now and check that everything was alright. The last time they had spoken, she had been quite upset with Pete over the divorce.

Lifting herself from the table she picked up her cup and carried it over to the sink. Phoebe felt a little sorry for Pete; after all, it *was* Sonia who had left him . . . . for Gary. Pete was obviously hurt by it all and doing his best to make the divorce difficult, but Sonia seemed so hard with him, as if he were a toy she had finished playing with. She couldn't understand why she had to be like that . . . . but, there again . . . . it was nothing to do with her. Anyway, she would call and see how she was today.

Wiping her hands, she collected the phone from its mounting, returned to the table and entered 'S' into the directory. Sonia's name flashed digitally onto the screen and Phoebe cleared her throat and pressed the OK button.

'Hello, Sonia, it's mum,' she chirped into the phone, her eyes scanning the ceiling.

'Oh, hi mum. That's strange, I was just thinking about you.'

'In the nicest possible way, I hope.'

'Yes, of course. It's your anniversary today, isn't it? . . . . happy anniversary!'

'Thank you, dear. Yes, thirty years today. It seems a very long time ago.'

'It must seem a very long time living with dad all those years.' Phoebe smiled, relieved to hear Sonia sounding more like her old self. 'How is he, by the way?'

'He's fine. Out at the moment, so I'm having a bit of peace and quiet. What about you? I was ringing to see how you are. Last time we spoke you were a bit harassed.'

'Well, I'm okay . . . . I suppose. This is one of my better days, which means I haven't heard anything from Pete for a while. He's just been so . . . . well, bloody-minded about the divorce. It makes me wonder how we ever lived together at all. I could scream at him sometimes.'

'Yes dear, but these things take time. I'm sure he'll come round eventually.'

'I want him to come round *now*, not eventually.'

'Try and take it easy . . . . no need for you to become so stressed because of it.' Phoebe stared out of the window and changed the phone to her other ear, wondering if she should have called at all; some things are best left alone. 'I'm sure everything will work out fine.'

'You are so optimistic, mother . . . . it would do Pete good to talk to you, then he might calm down a bit.'

Phoebe gulped. Perhaps it was Sonia, herself, who needed to calm down, but she didn't want to get involved and suitably changed the subject. 'I don't think so, dear. Pete was never one for listening too well. Anyway . . . . are you still coming round for lunch on Sunday? Neville is coming.'

'Err . . . . yes, I think so, but I wondered if I could bring Gary with me. It might be a good opportunity to introduce him to the family . . . . as long as dad isn't going to kick off and embarrass me.'

'I'm sure that will be fine, dear. It will be nice to meet him.' Phoebe wasn't sure how George would react, knowing full well how he had been acting recently . . . . but they had to meet Gary sometime.

'You'll just love him, mum, he's so sweet . . . . and he's dying to meet you.'

'Then that's settled. Come round about one o'clock and we can chat before lunch.'

'Okay, mum, that's great. Look, I'll have to go now, I'm meeting Neville for a sandwich. We'll see you on Sunday, have a lovely anniversary.'

'Oh, right, thanks . . . . we'll see you then . . . . bye.'

'Bye, mum.'

Phoebe sighed once again and pressed the red button to end the call. It should be an interesting Sunday afternoon. She hoped George would be good . . . . of course he would, she would speak to him before then.

She stood up, returning the phone to its mounting and flicked the switch on the kettle. Sonia seemed much better today, and after all these weeks, they would finally meet Gary. Well, it was bound to happen sooner or later.

She scowled as she thought about George again and glanced up at the kitchen clock. How strange . . . . it must have stopped, it was still showing five to twelve, she was sure George had only recently put a new battery in it. Never mind, she would remind him again when he got home. She poured the boiling water on to the teabag. Yes, that was very strange . . . .

. . . . 'Can you hear me, voice?' George glanced around as he spoke out.

'Yes, George.'

'What will I be like when I go back to my life?'

'What do you mean, exactly?'

'Well . . . . I mean . . . . will I be different . . . . different to how I was before?'

'That will depend on how you want to be.'

'But . . . . I feel different, here with you in this Library. And the things we are talking about . . . . well, they are already helping me see that I could be different.'

'This is the idea, George, to look at life and speak of the truth which lies behind your confusion. By doing this we will shed a little light onto certain aspects of your life you may wish to change. Remember life is not a sentence with fixed penalties - it is a continuous evolution of energies given to you to express yourself in the best way possible. It is entirely up to you when and how you would use these energies.'

'Yes, I am beginning to understand that there is more to life than I ever imagined, but I suppose my worry is that when I go back I will forget all this, and I will be the same as I was before.'

'You cannot forget, for the experience will be written deep into your soul. Once you start to question life, you will find that life will question you - always one step ahead, always guiding you further and further along the path. You do not have to try too hard to hear the voice of life beckoning you forward. It is but a whisper of willingness.'

'Yes, but what about you? How will I be able to hear your voice?'

'You will have to trust your feelings, George. When you start to observe the thought patterns of your mind, you will notice that most of it is made up of 'background noise'. This 'background noise', as I have called it, forms the day by day running of your life. For example, you may be going shopping and your thoughts thus will provide you with a list of goods you would like to purchase, or, you may be leaving for work and you may have to check yourself that everything you need is with you.

But, it is beyond this superficial thought process that the main focus of creation lies. It is at a deeper level of thought that the world you live in is created. I would liken this observation to a radio station that has to be 'tuned in'. First of all it is necessary to remove all the background static before you can hear the announcement. Are you with me so far?'

'Yes, I think I'm 'tuned in'.'

'Well, that's good. I'd hate you to blow a fuse. Now, it is here, at this deeper level, where you will make the bigger decisions regarding your life, so it is necessary that you quieten down the static interference. That is to say, it can only be observed in the silence, allowing the presence of your true self to arise. This is where you will find me. It is a moment of shutting down everything 'out there' and opening up to the truth within. Are you still with me?'

George scratched his head, surprisingly comfortable with the conversation. 'Yes, I'm fine.'

'Right, now you are in touch with your deeper emotional feelings, and it is here where you can touch the truth of your decisions. If you are feeling anxious or fearful about your way forward, then maybe it is time to check where your thoughts are coming from. You see, the highest thought you hold will be from me, and it will be a thought shrouded in love - with no compromise. If you are feeling emotional pain from your thoughts, then you are responding to life in a fearful manner.

You should not worry about it, George. As I have said, I am always with you, and if you have a mind to find me, then so you shall. Don't take life too seriously. Life is to be enjoyed, to be laughed at. Accept life and all that comes with it in the knowing that whatever happens, it will be for your own good.'

'But I do accept most things . . . . don't I?' George's mind was ticking over quickly, trying to think straight, he hadn't examined himself this closely before.

'Well, yes, you do accept the things that please you. Everybody can accept life if it is to their advantage, but it is the occurrences that you decide are no good for you that we should look at. The majority of things that come your way are looked at from a perspective of 'is this of benefit to me?' It is a judgement made by your perception which breaks down all occurrences into 'Good' or 'Bad', and naturally so. What you call good, will be accepted, but what you see as bad, will be rejected.

This is the reasoning of the conditioned, intellectual 'me' - to look at any situation or event and decide whether or not it can gain personally from it. It is a very narrow minded view, which creates a separation between what you see as your 'self' and the rest of humanity. It is a selfish attitude promoting a defence system against the rest of the world, leaving each individual isolated within their own personal quest for survival.'

'But nobody wants to accept things they don't feel are good . . . . things that are going to hurt. It is the human way to fight for what is best.'

'It is the human way to stand fast and defend against change. It is the human way to protect possessions up to the point of murder to ensure that its way of life is untouched. It is the human way to deny peace of mind and replace it with a fear that needs will be unmet. If you would only question the human way, then you would understand that it is your own thoughts creating the fear and perpetrating your action.

If, for a moment, you were to lay down your defences and accept that everything is happening for a purpose, then you may see that life can be kind to you. How many times do you have to struggle and fight against a situation, believing it to be a disaster in your life, only to look back on it and see that it brought you no harm, in fact, because of it, life had become easier?

In any situation where you perceive pain, where you are fearful of consequences hurting you, you should understand it is only your thoughts that are creating the problem. For you to then accept the situation knowing ultimately you cannot be hurt by anything external, would be to release those fears. It is only this acceptance that allows peace to rise within you. It is only through acceptance the true self will shine.'

'You make it sound very easy . . . . in reality, it is difficult to just accept everything.'

'What you say is perfectly true, George, it does take great practice and true devotion to accept a life of extreme difficulty. It is a process which may be slow at first, but it is a process which can begin by accepting the easier things that happen in your life. Accept that one day you may feel better than another. Accept that others will see life differently to you. Accept the cycles of nature which bring adverse weather to your daily routine. Accept that changes in your workplace will affect your way of life. Be willing to change and adapt your thinking when life becomes difficult. If you can try to flow with the changes in life, instead of adding resistance to them, you will see life will flow with you.'

Already, George could see this was where he was going wrong. He wanted everything in life to be just how he had planned it, he wanted everybody to behave the way he wanted them to behave . . . . and when things were different, he became annoyed.

'Do not expect life to remain the same forever. It is constantly changing as you evolve and create different situations for your self to experience. This is the only true constant of life: that it will constantly change. With or without your approval, it will change. These are the cycles of life, perfectly formed to bring you the exact experience at the exact time you need it. Your non-acceptance is a raging battle which prevents you from feeling at peace.

Of course, I am not saying you should accept any form of abuse, either physical or psychological. There are certain actions in life which no-one should have to endure and must be stopped.'

'What makes us fight so hard against change?' George stared down at his foot as he rotated his ankle, first one way, then the other. 'Why do we find it so difficult to accept?'

'Life is not too difficult to accept, if you would just stop judging it. This is the problem you have to overcome - Judgement means No Peace. You see, if you allow it, the conditioned self will stand as judge and jury over everything that happens in your life. But, not only that, it believes that the judgement it makes should be seen as wisdom.'

Rubbing at a scuff mark on his shoe, he reflected on the good advice he had given Sonia and Neville over the years. Surely it had been the right thing to do. He looked up, concern etched on his face. 'But, is it not true for me to say, that through life experience alone, I would be in a better position to judge than, say, a younger person?'

'This is exactly where the world becomes confused. You see, what is 'good' judgement to one can be 'bad' judgement to another, and the criteria you use to determine these categories will be inconsistent from one person to another. It is important for your own freedom, for your own peace of mind, to realise that not only should you *not* judge, but the truth is, you *cannot* judge. Judgement, for you *and* everybody else, *is impossible.*'

George was taken aback a little, now thinking he had done wrong.

'In order for you to judge anything correctly, you would have to be in a position to know an inconceivably wide range of facts. You would have to know the past, present and future details of everyone and everything involved within that judgement, and, consider the consequences of all minor details to a point that would make it impossible to contemplate at all. Not only that, but you would have to be certain that your perception of the situation would not be faulty, so that your judgement would be fair and honest to everyone concerned. This is a task that even the greatest of thinkers would regard as impossible.

All of you must remember how many times you thought you knew all the 'facts' you needed for judgement, and how wrong you were. Is there anyone who has not had this experience? Would you know how many times you thought you were right, without ever realising you were wrong? If you can understand what I am telling you, you can also understand that wisdom is not judgement. To be wise is to not judge at all; for judgement is the doorway to conflict.'

Again, George rubbed at his shoe, trying hard to cover up his embarrassment. He had always believed himself to be helping others with what he trusted was an experienced view of life, but perhaps he had been mistaken. 'Yes, I err . . . . see what you are getting at.'

'When you become open to the truth, you will find life is simple. It is only when you allow yourself to be blinded by the constant rumblings of thought that life becomes complicated. To forget about judgement will open the door to acceptance and when you accept, you will experience a new freedom allowing peace into your life. These are all simple steps you can take, eventually leading to the place you want to be - the place of the true self.'

'But I still have a problem with the fact that some people's lives must be so difficult to accept. What about people born with grave disabilities, how do they accept living under such conditions?'

'There will always be people who are living under circumstances which are difficult to accept. I am not saying acceptance brings you happiness. What I *am* suggesting is that acceptance will bring you peace, even though you are not 'happy' with your life conditions. If at all your circumstances are such that you cannot accept them, the way forward is to surrender as much as you can to your condition. Surrender to any external happening will *eventually* lead to acceptance. And so the cycle is this: surrender - acceptance - peace. This is the cycle which brings truth your way.'

'So . . . . I should just try to be more accepting of life?'

'If you did, George, life would become much easier for you. Why do you think you are irritable and bad tempered? Why do you find yourself tense and anxious with your family and friends? You could say 'it is this' or 'it is that' making life hard, but the truth is, it is your non-acceptance which creates an inner-resistance to life, leaving you fighting with yourself and everyone else. It is a decision you must make - to fight against the world, or allow yourself to flow with the beauty of it.'

George inhaled a big breath of air and brushed his hands over the silver strands of his hair. He could see that he wasn't doing himself any favours by fighting against life, always complaining and trying to change things to suit his way. He could see now that it was his own stupid attitude which made life so difficult.

'What you are looking for is a mind which is free of conflict, free from pain, anxiety and fear. The conditioned self, with all its images of conflict, has a centre which divides all relationships into 'me' and 'you'. But it is the understanding that deep relationship with another, free from the conditioned boundaries placed upon it, is the way of releasing your self-imposed imprisonment.

All this is an observation beyond the centre of your own little world, beyond the judgements and criticisms you have made which divide the world into fragments of self-justification. You cannot have peace outwardly, if your inner feeling is of mistrust.

Do you follow what I am saying, George? Perhaps it is not easy for you. Do you see that all your great problems in life are coming from a place within your own mind, which you, yourself, have cultivated and refined, shaped and styled into the entity you have called 'me'? It is quite amusing to know that you have then allowed this entity to control your every thought, decide your every action, to tell you what is right and what is wrong, dominating your life until you cannot look beyond its self-centred madness.

It is as if, as a child, you have taken an imaginary friend, a friend who goes everywhere with you and helps you to understand the ways of the world, a friend who says it loves you and wants to help you in any way it can to get the best out of life, a constant companion who tells you its only desire is for your welfare, and if you listen well . . . . one day you may be happy. But the companion has become the beast; the friend has become the monster . . . . the controlled has now become the controller. Can you see this, George?'

George wasn't sure he understood totally, but he nodded his head. He could at least see that something was making him unhappy, something was making life difficult for him. 'Yes . . . . err, there certainly is a problem somewhere.'

'To discover what it means to have a peaceful mind you must be free of this controller. But to do this, firstly, it is important for you to recognise this is happening. Once you can see for yourself the process of your erratic thoughts, and know it is this confusion which brings pain into your life, changes can be made. Quite simply, if you see something you don't like, stop doing it - it is as easy as that. The whole content of your consciousness is made up from all you are conditioned to believe.

This content is totally built from the past, and it is this past account of life which triggers thoughts. Never able to recognise anything new, these thoughts, consequently, are never free to expand.

The big question is: Can this content be emptied, and hence the mind be free to find a new way of thinking?'

' . . . .you tell me . . . . please.'

'I will, George. The answer is yes. A mind that holds no preconceived ideals becomes very spacious and new. A mind that is free becomes true unto itself - it is all a matter of perception. But can the mind see its own limitation, and understand such limitation has been placed upon it by external authority? If you can perceive the constraint within yourself, then the very seeing can release it.'

'Phew . . . . this is taking some thinking about.' George wiped his hands over his brow as he considered the conversation. 'Are you saying that to look beyond everything I have been taught is the way to open up my mind . . . . a new way to look at life?'

'Yes, I am indeed saying this. At the moment your mind is working within the confined space you have allowed it, and if it is questioned, will answer within the philosophy programmed to respond. Now, as I have said, if such a mind can be emptied of content, it becomes new and alive, with unlimited space for expansion. It becomes a boundless area of free perception, without opinions, without judgements, without conclusions and therefore without conflict.

Take your time and think about this, George. Ask yourself *why* you are so different from each other. If you think about it clearly, you will see the differences between humans are established by the individual content of each mind - your thinking is different due to individual belief, and therefore separation must occur with all its consequences. And so you may see, to release the content of such a self-centred mind, must also release the conflict you have cultivated between each other.'

Something inside George told him this was true, he didn't have to think too deeply about it. Everybody wanted life to suit their own needs and satisfy their own demands, each person with his own way of looking at life with individual expectations. It was because of these personal demands that life became complicated and the arguments started.

'All this may appear to be the most complex of issues to you, but again, there is a simplicity behind it, which, once discovered, will become very clear. Look at the boundaries you have set for yourself, observe the narrow space you have placed your world into, and you will start to realise how insecure it is. You believe yourself to be safe and protected behind your ideals and philosophies, whilst you are angry and discontented with everything which lies outside them. Obviously, this is not a good way to live.'

Again, George examined his own mental state. The truth was he did get annoyed when he was confronted with anything outside his own belief system and acted angrily against things which were not his concern.

'Everything happens for a purpose and even though it may not be happening for you personally, someone, somewhere, will be learning and evolving from that happening. This is what you must accept: that each soul is progressing around and beyond his or her own level of evolution, experiencing life along their own pathway. When you know this, then you also know that for you to judge will bring the pain which comes with non-acceptance. Let the world live, and you may live with it. This is a bold statement of truth which allows you the freedom of living.

Remember who you are and why you are here. It is your great purpose upon the earth to evolve, to let the light of who you are shine out into the world with honesty and understanding. When you start to release the chains with which you have bound yourself and feel peace rising up inside, you will know in your heart you have recognised something you cannot let go of.

It is a feeling that cannot be compared to anything you have made in your outer world. It is a feeling that, with just a little willingness, will grow into a tidal wave of happiness. This is the love of the true self reaching out from the place you have hidden it, stretching out its golden light for all to see. When you can feel this love, you are ready to move forward. When you can feel this love, *you are ready to forgive*. . . . .

. . . . Phoebe was not happy. Her trip to the bathroom revealed the mess George had left . . . . shampoo spilled on the edge of the bath, hair in the plughole, soap scum dried hard around the white enamel base.

She checked the sink to find toothpaste splashed and left to dry hard on the chrome-plated taps, it was so typically thoughtless of him. She pursed her lips . . . . he knew one of the rules of the house was to keep the bathroom tidy, she had said it enough times for him to remember. He was hopeless. The last thing she wanted to do today was to clean up after him.

Storming into the bedroom, she removed her silk dressing gown and threw it onto the bed, reaching out for her clothes from the chair. She finished buttoning up her blouse, breathing deeply at her reflection in the dressing table mirror until her anger started to subside. Maybe she could excuse him today . . . . after all, it was a special day for them. 'Let it go Phoebe, it's not the end of the world.' She spoke softly to herself as she walked back into the bathroom.

Hands on hips, she thought of him at the meeting, hoping it was going well and then reluctantly opened the cupboard, found the bathroom cleaner and set about her task.

FORGIVE THE
<u>INNOCENT</u>

'Give them your love, but not of your ways,
give them your time, but not all your days,
give them your truth, but they will decide,
the bit that they want, the bit that they hide.'

Adam Katowycz opened his bleary eyes and sat up in bed. He looked at the clock; it was nine fifty-five. His gaze fell onto the crumpled packet of cigarettes lingering on top of his bedside table next to the matches and half-filled glass ashtray. He reached out, taking one from the packet and lit it, drawing deeply to inhale the smoke into his system.

The first smoke of the day felt good to him, he could sense the vapours filling his body. First his chest and stomach, then down through the veins in his arms with a wave of pleasure touching his whole body bit by bit, reaching every part with its gift of relaxation. Now he felt better, more alive.

Reaching up to his right, he pulled the faded blue curtains back a little to allow some daylight into the room and opened the small window, exhaling the smoke from his lungs with a breath of ecstasy. It was murky outside, with a thick drizzly rain falling down from a heavy sky. He fell backwards, propping himself up on his pillow and took another long, slow draw from the cigarette.

Adam was seventeen years old, and, like most seventeen year old boys, thought he knew enough about life to look after himself. He didn't need the brainwashing of school anymore. Who were they to tell *him* how to get by in life? You had to be clever, smarter than the system to beat the system. How was algebra or reading Shakespeare going to help him make money? Adam knew better than that, he'd learned his lessons on the street - the hard way. He knew what he wanted and he knew how to get it.

He pushed his cigarette again to his lips and took a big pull, watching it glow and burn as he blew smoke rings towards the open window. Anyway, he didn't fit in at school, he didn't agree with the pathetic rules and regulations and domineering teachers trying to tell him what to do, they could only see things one way, which was to work hard for qualifications and get yourself a decent job before you could earn good money.

He had laughed long and hard at their wimpish remarks. He had made more money in a week selling drugs than they could earn in a month. Now that was a clever occupation . . . . the kids wanted them - somebody had to supply them - why not him? Why shouldn't he be the one to profit? It was a simple equation of supply and demand equals take the money and run. What use was geography and physics? He had told them what they could do with great certainty.

Adam twisted his wiry body, throwing his legs around to sit on the side of the bed. He sucked out the last smoke from his cigarette and stubbed it out aggressively in the dirty ashtray. Today he would do something exciting, something to kill his boredom. He pulled on his well-worn jeans and sweatshirt and noisily made his way downstairs to make a cup of coffee, whistling the same tune he had taken to bed with him the night before, singing the few words he could remember and making up others as he jumped down the stairs two at a time.

There was nobody else in the house to disturb, his mother had gone to work long ago and anyway, he didn't care about her. She was always picking on him, trying to change him, telling him he should do something with his life. Why should he when he was happy enough just doing whatever he wanted?

His song changed to a whistle again as he reached the cluttered kitchen and switched on the kettle. He opened the cupboard door and reached for a mug, putting coffee and sugar into it. As he waited for the water to boil, his eyes fixed on a scrap of paper on the worktop, he picked it up and started to read. *'No cereal left, go to shop and buy some, I've left money in tin, also please do washing up.'* Adam looked at the untidy sink piled high with pans and plates. He screwed up the note and tossed it into the bin, scowling as he poured water into his mug. He could feel the swell of anger rising up inside. 'Why can't she just leave me alone?' He spat out the words in annoyance, furiously stirring his coffee and threw the dirty spoon to join the top of the pile in the sink.

His dark eyes darted across the kitchen, picking out the red and green pizza box he had brought home last night. He remembered saving a piece for his breakfast and his mood lightened a little as he collected it, picked up his coffee and walked steadily back upstairs again, whistling his song.

Adam put down his coffee on the small bedside table and laid his congealed ham and mushroom pizza carefully on the bed. He crawled across his duvet to pull open his curtains wider for maximum light, staring out of the window for a while at the miserable scene, and then jumped back down to eat his breakfast and slurp on his coffee. He was still tired, still yawning, feeling the pinch of his many late nights. His jacket, shoes and socks were dumped in a pile across the bedroom floor, and a smile of remembrance unfolded across his face as his eyes rested on them.

His thoughts shifted back towards his mother; he needed to get away from her, to find his own place to live. He wanted his freedom . . . . and she was the one taking it from him. She was the one who still thought of him as a child. His mood changed again as frustration wiped away the smile from his face. He would save up his money and get his own place, that way, without her, he could double his drug business.

He had plans for the future, and they didn't include her. She had lied to him, she had told him his father was a good man who cared about him, but they were all lies, his father had run off, back to Poland, ten years ago. How could he be a good man? How could he care? Adam had a vague recollection of a drunken man always pushing his mother around, how could that be seen as concern for his family. Anyway, it was a long time ago, he was grown now and could look after himself. He could get by without him . . . . without anybody. He shoved the last crust of pizza into his mouth and reached out for his drink.

Adam had his own philosophy on life, which was to take whatever you can when you can and never mind anybody else. He slid his mug back across the table and stared expectantly around the room looking for inspiration,. 'Yes!' he cried out and suddenly leapt from the bed and turned on his games' console, positioning himself enthusiastically in front of his new-found interest. The monitor screen came to life with a burst of light and a quiet jingle of electronic music. He waited patiently as his arousal heightened.

In no time the screen flashed up *Ready to Load* and he quickly injected the disc into the machine, waiting to hear the click and recognition of his choice. He took a moment to collect and light a cigarette, drawing heavily on it and then placing it down into the overflowing ashtray which he carried back to his station and rested carefully on the edge of the bed. He took another draw, exhaling the smoke towards the window as the monitor told him *War Games - Ready to Play,* he clicked *Continue* and dropped the cigarette back into the ashtray.

'Right, here we go . . . . level three I think,' he spoke menacingly to the machine and double clicked on his choice, tapping his fingers on the table as he waited for his challenge to emerge. He was good at this, with quick reactions, giving him a head start when dodging the spray of bullets fired at the animated figure he had become.

Weaving himself in and out of the trees, he retaliated with a sharp burst of fire to clear his path. Zap - zap - zap, he muscled his way through jungles of heavy armaments, across deserts of sand mines, up and along dark mountains of desperate attack. He was good. He could clear them all. His score clicked higher and higher as he counted the casualties: eight, nine, ten men so far and him without a scratch, without even a near miss. 'Yes!' he called out and pushed himself deep into a clearing: eleven, twelve.

He was on a roll now, blitzing his surroundings with grenades and machine gun, crawling low across the ground and rising up with a barrage of bullets to protect his life, and then running wildly back through the trees with figures bursting out in front of him, left and right. They screamed with pain as he laid them out, one at a time. He was strong and powerful, angry with his weapons. 'Yes . . . . yes!', another round fired, another body fallen. He ducked his head and ran into a wooden building marked *Safe Haven*.

Adam stopped for a while and breathed deeply, stretching across for his cigarette burning away in the ashtray. He inhaled a final time and stubbed it out, reaching for the packet to light up again. Taking another deep breath he shifted his eyes back to the screen and with a whistle of delight on his lips, clicked on the button marked *Attack* . . . .

. . . . Catherine Katowycz stood upright, stretching her back and inspected the tiled area of floor she had spent the last fifteen minutes cleaning. It looked good enough to her, even sparkling a little in the brightness of the office lights, but then, it was still wet, and always did look better with a wet sheen. She was later than usual today, just managing to finish the ground floor before the workers had arrived, but now she had caught up a little and had almost finished the seminar room for tomorrow morning.

Catherine was forty-two years old, but today, with the heaviness of her mind, felt as if she were seventy-two. No matter how many times she told herself not to worry, she still couldn't let it go.

Her great problem was with her son, Adam, and why they couldn't live together without so much disagreement. She had practiced the words she would say to him, each time in a different way, but always with a plea for them to be friends, always with a hope that they could love each other. He was her boy. He was her life . . . . past, present and future. He was her hopes and dreams, all tied together into one package, but now he had left her cold with his thoughtless attitude.

She had tried long and hard to communicate with him, it was right for mother and son to love and help each other . . . . surely he could see she was doing her best? Perhaps his age was to blame, and when he got a bit older, when he had left his teenage years behind, *then* he would love her.

Wiping her damp brow with the back of her hand, she pushed the mop once again into the galvanised metal bucket and sighed a little as she continued with her work. It could have been different if Yvan had still been around. If he had only stayed . . . . they would have been a family, doing things together, as families do, and Adam would have had a father figure to look up to. He had loved his dad and so wanted to be like him . . . . but now all he felt was resentment.

She paused for a moment to brush away the loose strands of dark hair falling into her eyes and considered her situation. It had been difficult for her too. She was the one who had been deserted and left alone to bring up a child. Ten years of hard work with little money and no help from anywhere had not been easy. She should be proud . . . . proud of her achievement. But where was her child now? Drifting away from her bit by bit.

She glanced down at her left hand. Still, the tiny gold wedding ring placed on her third finger, a little tighter now with the passing of the years, but even after all this time, she couldn't bring herself to take it off. Maybe she had taken strength from it, a silent surge of energy giving her a union of hope, a blessing that someone else was with her to help her through life. Maybe her love was still with Yvan. Could she admit it to herself now, ten years on? She sighed again, pressing the mop firmly into the grid. Anyway, it didn't matter, he wouldn't come back now, he had said as much in his last letter.

She dropped the wet mop back to the floor as her thoughts returned to Adam, he was the one she was losing now. It was her biggest fear . . . . that he would leave her and not return, he was such a stubborn boy, even at school, the teachers were troubled by him. They had written to her saying he was impossible to teach. But that was wrong . . . . Adam was a good kid, he just needed a bit of patience and understanding, they couldn't possibly know him as well as she did, he was just . . . . he was just confused. She had pleaded with him to try harder, to try again, but he still wouldn't go back to finish his education.

Catherine fumbled around her neck and grasped the silver crucifix hanging there. She held it tightly for a moment and took a deep breath. Everything would be alright. Another hour and she would be finished with work, then she could go home and talk to Adam. Maybe they could try and get to the bottom of his problems. He should settle down and get a job . . . . then he would feel better about himself. Her confidence grew the more she thought about it, but, she would have to be careful with him and find the right words to say . . . .

. . . . Beep, beep - beep, beep. The mobile phone flinched and lit up on Adam's bedside table. He groaned and slowly moved his concentration from the game to fix his eyes on to the interrupting text. He quickly turned back to face the screen, but it was too late, he was doomed; shot through the head by a well camouflaged sniper hidden deep within the leafy branches of a tree. Slamming down the control, he scrambled over to the phone and picked it up, hitting 'receive' with his nicotine stained finger as the message glowed '*Can u do me stuff 4 tnite*'.

The text was a nuisance, but, it meant business was good. Adam instantly pressed out his reply. '*Yeh, no prob will c u bout 7*'. He pushed on the 'send' button and fell heavily down onto his bed, leaning over to collect his cigarettes, matches and ashtray, placing them carefully down beside him. Peering into the cigarette packet, he felt a little stab of panic, realising he only had three left and would have to fetch some more. He lifted one out and lit it, inhaling deeply to steady the adrenalin still coursing through his body. Business was good, he had built up quite a few customers already, and it could only get better.

Feeling much calmer, he rolled over onto his back and stared at the ceiling with the cigarette dangling from his mouth. He exhaled and watched the smoke rise, dancing like a cloud of mist along a river bed, gracefully spreading across the discoloured paintwork of his room. He closed his eyes for a moment and wondered what he would do when he was rich. Get his own place for sure. Buy a nice car . . . . not too big . . . . but a fast black one with smoky glass. He would have a house in the sun where he could hide away when he needed a break . . . . and a wine rack, full of the finest wines . . . . although, he had never drunk wine before. He laughed at his thrilling dream. He would have a gold chain and dark sunglasses to make him look cool and mysterious, like a spy.

His eyes sprung open. But he had to be careful . . . . he had to be clever . . . . smarter than the cops.

He laughed again and drew on his cigarette, trying unsuccessfully to hit the ceiling with smoke rings as the curtains billowed from the gusty draught of the open window. Staying one step ahead of the law was the key to his success. He had to be shrewd and quick witted to reap his reward. Pulling himself upright again, he quenched his thirst with the last cold dregs of coffee and stabbed out his cigarette.

A contented smile played on his lips, as he again started to whistle the tune that wouldn't leave him alone . . . .

. . . . 'The world has become separated and disjointed, built up from different parts, all put together by eyes that see space between everything and then calls each object by an individual name. Whatever is looked upon is given its own identification and purpose. That, in itself, George, is a task of huge magnitude which makes it appear you are separate from every other living thing, in fact, everything you see is the exact *same* energy of the universe. What you see is an outer appearance shaped according to its vibrational frequency. This energy is recognized to be different, and is given a separate name. It is this vast illusion of self-deception which allows the conditioned self to compare and isolate itself from the rest of the world.

You see, when you look at a tree, you will see exactly that . . . . a tree. This is something you have learned to do since you were a young child. You have been told that a certain shaped image which holds various characteristics is to be called . . . . a tree. Can you imagine how many different objects you have done this with? It has taken many years for you to learn each symbol individually and give it a separate name.

This is the way of your world. A way of separation. Is it any wonder that when you come to look at each other you will use the exact same formula which has served you so well – look at the image and give it a name? It is the way you separate everything from your 'self'. When you have done this, it becomes easy for you to judge what you see and categorise it into good or bad, like or dislike. You do not understand any other way of living because, as a child, the world has taught you this is how it should be done.'

'But I can't see what is so wrong with this. Surely children have to learn and recognise a tree when they see one, they have to know the names of different objects around them, they have to be able to differentiate between things. How else could it be . . . . how would we communicate? We have to recognise each other and call each other by different names . . . . or else . . . .'

'What you say is perfectly true, George, the world would be a very strange place without some form of identification. However, the point I am trying to make goes much deeper than a visual interpretation. It is one thing to look around and acknowledge all you see with a respectful identification, a name you have given to the image, but it is quite a different matter when you believe yourself to be completely separate from it. Let me explain a little more.

When a child is born it is completely devoid of any worldly knowledge. It is pure and innocent, without any care which may detract from its loving nature. If it feels discomfort in any way, needs feeding or cleaning, it will certainly let you know by voicing its displeasure, but it cannot reason as to why it is uncomfortable, it behaves in a very basic, instinctive way.

At this stage of development, the child has no more needs than to be looked after in the most pleasant way possible, it is some time later that the child suddenly becomes more aware of its environment. It starts to ask questions of the outer world it has been born into, developing a great hunger for knowledge.

The child has found its intelligence, a consciousness of itself and everything surrounding it. This intelligence, as we have already discussed, is the intellectual centre, which all parents would agree, gives the child its own personality. I know you will understand this, George.'

'Yes, I remember my own two children growing up. Sonia, that's my eldest . . . . well, of course, you know . . . . she was very forward in her ways, she always seemed quite advanced for her age . . . . although Neville was very self conscious and shy with other children . . . .' George became silent as his thoughts drifted back to those early years. It had been a 'special' time in his life and he had fond memories, he loved his kids dearly and the pain of missing them made him ache inside.

'It's okay, George, I know how you feel, but don't worry, all will be well.'

Again, he was comforted by the voice's caring words and managed to steady his emotions.

'Let us try and continue . . . . parents are filled with pride as they watch their children develop and build up a memory of visual remembrance, expanding their intelligence by learning new words in the most outstanding way.'

Now George could allow himself a little smile. He and Phoebe had been so proud and excited to watch their children develop. He recalled coming home from work and discussing the progress they had made, anything new they had done or said would fill them with delight.

'I can see you are with me on this, it certainly is a wonderful time for all parents, but it is also the time when the child is most open to external influences. Firstly the child takes on board the whims and ideals of the parents, and soon discovers that to be 'good' is to be rewarded, but to be 'bad' is to be punished. It learns to follow certain traditions of culture which become apparent as it begins to integrate with others outside the family environment.

The child starts to form a basic profile of itself, and becomes educated as to what is expected from it as it grows. It builds a moral code based upon suggestion and environmental rules and regulations, adding its own prejudices along the way . . . . and then suddenly, one day, you notice the innocent child is gone.'

'Yes, but this is all part of growing up. We have to teach our children the 'rights' and 'wrongs' of the world, we have to prepare them for what is ahead . . . . surely this is the right way to do it.'

'But what is it you are preparing them for, George? What is it you would have your children believe at such an early age? Are you teaching them that life is a flow of natural energy, a warmth of truthful, honest approach, or do you tell them that life is a competition to be won at all costs? After all, you have already planted a seed of deceit into your child's mind by telling him that obedience is good, and if he follows the rules he may reap his reward.

As each generation moves into the next, it is the same old story, the same conditions laid down firmly for the child to follow: 'Do it this way and everything will be fine', or 'stick to the rules and life may not be too bad'. All this you have told your children because all this you were told yourselves. Is this what you mean by preparing them for what is ahead, by telling them of the harshness of the world?'

George was taken aback a little, he had never thought about it from this point of view. Of course children were vulnerable in the early stages of life, they trusted all they were told as being correct, it was up to the parents to be honest with them . . . . but if the parents were mistaken in their understanding of life, the same philosophy would be passed on.

'You see the developing intelligence, the intellect, is not just content with building up a storehouse of names and identities, it wants much more than this. The intelligence also begins to look around and gather information about other children. It takes notice of different developing personalities alongside its own, and analyses what it sees from a new self-centre of observation.

This self-centre, even though still in the steps of infancy, quickly decides what it likes and does not like, and may become quite a stubborn, almost uncontrollable force within the child, as a lot of parents have discovered to their dismay. The sweet natured, loving, passive child has now become the opposite, without care or compassion for anything but itself.'

Again, George allowed his thoughts back to his own children. He recalled how wonderful they both were up to the age of around four years old . . . . . . and then something seemed to happen . . . . both Sonia and Neville started to rebel and argue against himself and Phoebe, but mostly with each other, but wasn't this a natural process of the children growing up? After all every child was the same. He coughed, clearing his throat. 'Yes, I err . . . . see what you mean.'

'You see, children are hurt by parents, hurt by society and education which all compare them to their siblings and other children, creating conflict in a world which will only accept a winner as a strong human being.

Can you imagine the confusion within a child's mind as it battles constantly against conflicting ideals and morals, forever having to prove itself beyond inadequacy? Is there any wonder a child becomes violent and rebels against this strange foundation for life?

Take a look at the new generation, spending their time playing virtual reality computerised games which glamorize everything that is destroying your society. War games teaching children it is good to be tough, it is powerful to kill, driving them forward with a desire to win at all costs, taking away any signs of compassion or humility.

This is their new education, which shows no mercy to anyone who stands in their way. Other computerised games glamorize life on the streets with gang warfare, drugs and knife crimes. It is all there for you to see; in every bedroom of the next generation you are able to view the future of your society . . . . and it does not look too clever.

You allow your children to feel the backlash of your broken relationships, the anger and violence you show to each other when your needs and expectations have been broken, using your children as a prop to hurt and 'get back' at your failed partnership.

From the moment they start their schooling, pressure is applied so heavily on them that, by the time they are teenagers, their self-esteem has been crushed under the burden of having to be best, until some have become quite suicidal. They are lonely young people spending their days desperately trying to end their pain with a great wanting for money and material gain, hoping this will put an end to their misery . . . . and, of course, most children make the grade and manage to fit into society's ways by working hard and acquiring good jobs, bringing a little stability into their lives. They are able to follow the blueprint for success laid in front of them as children and believe they have achieved everything that their parents and society have expected from them.

But there are others who cannot cope with the external pressures of life, there are those who through class systems, low intelligence or poor education are abandoned and placed into categories of failure, destined to live their lives as second class citizens.

Can it be right and proper to treat your children in this way, when all they have done is fallen short of an ideal . . . . which, in the first place, was never intended as true?

This cannot be what you want for your children, all of you, without exception, would have a much better world for them to grow up in.'

In many cases George could see this was happening. There *was* a gulf in society that opened up and pushed out the ones who were judged to be inadequate and from a personal point of view, he was pleased that his own kids were doing fine. Shaking his head in despair, he readily agreed. 'Of course, we must change this . . . . but how?'

'It is a matter of some concern, but even through the misguided actions of your world, there are still times when you may look at your children and recognise the same innocent beauty which lifted your hearts when they were young. There are times when you can still touch upon those special feelings of love which allow you to see all is not lost. The child may have changed, but only portrays a false, conditioned image. Beneath the surface is still the oneness of energy connecting each and every human being to a unity of togetherness which cannot be broken.

This is what we must discuss . . . . this is what you must find again to change your world' . . . .

*'And I did know that the mirror in my heart
did cast a mighty reflection.'*

Gazing intently into the bathroom mirror, Adam Katowycz applied gel to his raven hair, pulling each strand until he was pleased with the reflection staring back at him. He looked mean and moody as he lowered his dark eyebrows, his youthful good looks gave him confidence to go out into the world with an arrogance to make things happen, he knew he wouldn't get anywhere by being shy and nervous.

Pleased with his image, he started to whistle as he twisted his head around to double check the back of his hair. His mirrored grin widened as he imagined himself in the life he would love to lead as a racing driver. He practised in the mirror and started to laugh, *'Brrrrrr . . . . Brrrrrr, Katowycz stepping up through the gears and screeching on the brakes as he zips himself down through the pits and back onto the circuit leading the field round the final bend and into the straight.'* He announced himself onto the podium as he reached out to collect his prize. *'And once again, the winner of this year's Grand Prix . . . . Adam Katowycz.'* He could hear the crowd roar with approval as he popped the cork on the huge bottle and squirted the champagne high into the air.

Adam had always wanted to drive a fast car. He could drive, he had picked it up just by watching, just by riding along in the passenger seat, taking notice. That's how clever he was, only needing to see something once to know how it was done. He remembered when he was only fifteen, an older friend had let him drive his car and accelerate up to high speeds. It had been great fun, he was a natural driver . . . . his friend had said as much.

Swivelling one more time to appreciate himself, he screwed the top back on the tub of gel, tossed it into the bathroom cabinet and strode back to his bedroom, pulling out another cigarette from the packet in his jeans pocket. His last cigarette. He lit it, blowing a slow continuous stream of smoke towards the open window. He grimaced at the view, knowing he would have to go out to buy some more and it was still raining with a heavy drizzle descending out of the dismal sky . . . . but at least he wouldn't have to see his mother.

He glanced at the black digital clock on his bedside table, ten fifty-six. He knew she would come home from work soon and he didn't want to be around when she did . . . . she would only aggravate him again. He imagined, yet again, being away from here without her to spoil his freedom. His thoughts raced ahead . . . . maybe he would buy her a gift at Christmas and call round to see her on birthdays . . . . just to show her how well he was doing. If she could see how happy he was, then she would have to leave him alone. He stared out towards the pattering rain as his vision took shape, still aware it was his last cigarette.

Suddenly, he knew where he could get some more, he remembered his mother's hidden supply in her secret drawer where she kept her jewellery. She had stopped smoking a while ago, but she always kept some for emergencies, for the times when she couldn't cope. He didn't miss much in this house. He felt pleased with himself and relaxed a little, finishing his smoke with pleasure.

Stubbing it out, he jumped swiftly from the bed, whistling loudly with the shrill sound of a blackbird before nightfall as he made his way into his mother's bedroom.

He knelt down and reached underneath her bed, pushing aside the piles of discarded shoes, and whistled higher with sounds of delight, as he pulled out a battered brown leather box, divided into two drawers, each with a small brass handle. He gently pulled open the top one to reveal the treasure he was hoping for . . . . a half-full packet. She wouldn't miss a couple of those, and anyway, he didn't care too much whether she did or not.

Lifting out the packet, he removed two cigarettes and dropped them on the floor behind him, replacing it neatly, smiling at his cleverness as he started to close the drawer, but then opened it again as his eyes fixed on a small, light blue envelope with a red and white edging, stamped neatly on the corner *'Airmail'*. He stared at it for what seemed like an age, he knew it could only be from his father.

87 'Whatever Happened to George?'

Slowly taking it out, his heart fluttered a little, raising its beat . . . . sensing something wasn't quite right. She hadn't told him she'd received a letter. She hadn't mentioned anything about it. But he was curious . . . . he had to know what was in it. It was from his father. He had a right. He opened it cautiously, with a feeling of dread and started to read.

Dear Catherine,

It has been a long time now since we have spoken to each other. I hope you are well and that life is being kind to you. It has been difficult for me over the last few years, but finally I have managed to stop drinking. That is, I haven't had a drink now for almost a year, and I am feeling much better for it. It has been a hard road, with many setbacks and many times my mind has wilted and taken me back to the heavy days of alcohol, but at the moment my mind is clear.

Catherine, I am writing to you today to tell you I have met someone else. She is a Polish girl who lives close to where I work and our friendship has become very strong. We have lived together for six months and she has helped me greatly with my drinking problem. I know this may not surprise you after all these years, but it is now I must ask you for a divorce from our marriage. When I think of the time we were together, and the boy – it is still a difficult thing to do, but we have to move on and it is my time to do that. I have instructed a lawyer about our circumstances and he will write to you with papers for you to sign. I had always hoped we could still be friends as our memories keep us together. How is Adam? I know he will be growing up and soon will be a man. I do care about him and one day hope I will be able to see him, and will try to send you some money to help. I hope you will be able to understand.

Love Yvan.

Adam slowly knelt up on the carpet, breathing deeply as he finished reading his father's letter. He checked the date on the envelope . . . . it was two years' old, and she hadn't thought to mention it to him. He clenched his fists, feeling the agony of rejection again, reliving the pain of false promises made by his father. How could he care when he hadn't tried to see him once in all this time?

His hands were shaking as he read the letter again. His memories stretched to read the words of a man he could barely remember, a man who had deserted him so many years ago. He loved him, but he hated him. He wanted to see him . . . . but that was not possible. His father had made the decision for him. He could feel anger churning at his stomach, twisting around in his head. That man didn't care about him . . . . it was obvious from his writing. It was clear now to Adam . . . . he was on his own.

He slid the letter back into the envelope and returned it to the box, pushing it roughly back behind the shoes, picked up the cigarettes and walked sullenly to his room. He fell down onto his bed, clasping his arms around his knees, listening for a while to the faint sound of traffic and staring at the insistent patter of raindrops hitting his windowpane. The letter had told him nothing new, it just confirmed what he already knew . . . . he hated them . . . . both of them.

Lighting one of his mother's cigarettes, he scoured the room for his black hooded jacket, he needed to go out now to clear his head. He wanted to have some fun . . . . and with a flash of brilliance, he knew exactly what he would do. He would take a car . . . . and drive it fast . . . .

. . . . Catherine Katowycz opened the creaky door of the small janitor's room to store away the mop and bucket and folded up the bright yellow dusters, placing them neatly into the drawer for another day. She lifted her heavy winter coat from the peg and wrapped it tightly around her, taking care to fasten each button to protect herself from the adverse weather outside. Pulling the door behind her and after carefully locking it and making sure the key was safely inside her coat pocket, she picked up her umbrella and canvas bag from the floor and gladly made her way down the three flights of stairs to the giant revolving doors which allowed her access to the busy road outside. She waved goodbye to the receptionist as she halted for a moment to raise her umbrella against the gusty rain before stepping out.

Catherine had been waiting all morning for the time she could leave to go home and speak to Adam, but now it had arrived, she could feel the pull of anxiety tumbling around her stomach. All morning she had been thinking about it, choosing carefully the words she would say, planning the moment she would embrace her son and talk with him openly until they were close again. By mid-morning she had known exactly what she was going to say, but now it was gone - all mixed up in the nervous tension consuming her mind, raising again the doubts she had earlier dispelled.

She pushed her umbrella out in front to shelter her face from the sharp blasts of rain and set off slowly along Wadsworth Road trying to clear her thoughts with each step. She knew she had to be calm and talk to Adam in a friendly way. She would show some interest and ask him what he was doing today, that was a good start, a normal conversation between mother and son, maybe then they could talk about other things, things that were causing upset between the two of them.

She began to feel a little lighter as she walked briskly along, watching the traffic stopping and starting, slowly making its way through the miserable day. She waited patiently for the green man to tell her to go, before crossing and taking the footpath directing her away from the main road and on towards the house she had once shared with Yvan.

Again, her mind opened up the past. It would have been so different with him around. He was strong. He would have known what to say to Adam . . . . and Adam would have listened. She took a deep breath and her pace slowed a little as she considered, once again, telling her son about the divorce. After all, it had been nearly two years since she had signed the papers, and there was nothing she could do to change it now.

As she made her way slowly up the hill, she began to feel a little stronger and less alone, as if Yvan were somehow with her, telling her everything would work out. She had noticed it before, whenever she thought of him, she felt more able to make decisions. Today was no exception. Undoing her top button, she reached deep inside her coat and clutched again at the crucifix hanging around her neck, releasing a deep sigh as she let it go.

Catherine stopped momentarily on the footpath in front of her wrought iron gate, fumbling about in her bag to locate her key. She pulled down the umbrella, flicking off the rain as she reached the door and pushed the key into the lock.

'Adam, I'm home . . . . are you there?' she shouted, stepping into the hallway - but there was no reply. She tried again. 'Adam, are you there?' But the silence told her he wasn't . . . .

. . . .'Now . . . . for you to find and understand this energy of oneness, it becomes apparent that many barriers of pain, which have been built up over the years, have to be removed.' The voice filled the great hall of the Library in deep, crisp tones. 'It is clear, from self observation, that what you seek to find does not live within the intellectual, instinctive regions of the mind, but is something beyond the diminutive centre of the 'self'.

Over the years man has accumulated so many scars, so much hurt, that it becomes extremely difficult to look beyond the collectiveness of his darkened mind. He has built a wall around himself in order not to be hurt, and consequently spends his entire life hiding behind it, reliving past occurrences which have made him fearful of a better future.

The question to ask yourself is this, George: Is it possible for man to look beyond these hurts which produce all kinds of imbalance and find himself some form of sanity again? However, to find the answer, it is firstly important to discover exactly what it is that creates his torment. We have already established that man has developed a self centre, a place of intellectual prowess through which he observes his outer world, but what exactly does he see through this centre and what is the driving force behind it?

If you examine the content of the self, you will see that it is made up from a series of past events and consequences of those events which have made up the fundamental content of your life. What you see is a recollection of the past, a memory of thoughts and images which are all part of who you have become. I am sure you will agree with this George.'

Thinking about it carefully, he really had to agree, surely everybody *was* an accumulation of everything that had ever happened to them. 'Yes . . . . I can see this is true.'

'It is quite an incredible form of intelligence that can hold and process all the data and images it has come across during a lifetime of operation, and I would suggest that it is very much taken for granted, or by now you would have clearly seen the flaw in its credibility.'

Not wanting to appear ignorant about this matter, even though he really wasn't sure what the flaw was exactly . . . . George allowed himself a nod of the head.

'All kinds of experiences are locked away and held within the storehouse of yesterday. Everything you have called 'good' or 'bad' with various images of pleasure and pain indelibly stamped into the centre of the self which chews them over and gives them nourishment, or spits them out for a different image which it considers better.

This is the way of the mental consciousness of man, forever comparing, forever analyzing the data it sees, forever strengthening its position against what it believes to be a threat to its existence. All this is the field of thought creating a belief system about its 'self', promoting images of how it will relate to the world - and then defending those images with an emotional stockade of self-protection.'

George nodded his head again, but this time he was beginning to see the truth of it.

'But thought is also the trigger mechanism for pain. It digs deep into the mind, remembering past hurts, recalling past grievances, and brings them into a present time where it can relive the memory and experience the emotion again. If you were hurt yesterday, or a thousand yesterdays ago, thought will remind you gladly, by returning the conflict back into your mind.

The same pattern emerges when thought seeks out pleasure; it remembers pleasurable times of the past and judges present day life as a measure of yesterday's happiness.

This is how thought creates an appearance of time, by placing everything into a category of past, present and to come, but careful consideration of this psychological event will show you everything actually happens in the moment of now. Time is but a mental reflection of who you used to be projected to a future vision of who you would like to become. Of course, clock time has given you further belief that this illusion is real. You could say, George, that life has become a very 'narrow minded' affair.'

George had heard people say there was no such thing as time before . . . . but to him it made no sense at all. Everything he did was governed by time in one way or another . . . . but he did recognise the fact that thought gave an illusion of time . . . . *and* that everything happened in the present moment. It was a difficult concept for him to totally understand but he decided to continue with the dialogue. 'So time has become a big problem for us?'

'This is certainly a major part of your problems, you are living within a thought system which is never satisfied with life and is constantly striving for something more as and when it changes the images it sees. Through thoughts, the mind gathers friends of similar mind characteristics and rejects others who have a different outlook on life. It is a circle of deceit, bringing constant unease to a mind which is self contained within closed parameters.'

'And our thoughts are conditioned by all you have said before.'

'Excellent, George, we are making good progress. The mind is conditioned to believe that certain things are true, therefore, your thoughts, which make up the content of the mind, are also bound by the same process. Outwardly your thoughts create a world which is based upon these educated beliefs, whilst inwardly, they form an image of who you are in relation to this. To put it another way, what you believe to be reality is, in fact, a world of your own making. The moment you judge or translate what is seen, it is distorted according to your background. This being the case, how is it possible for you to even begin to see reality? How is it possible for you to find the truth of life?'

George was now able to see there was a problem here and even wanted to add to the conversation. It was strange for him to be philosophical, it was something he wasn't used to, but he was doing his best. 'So to find a true reality we have to release the preconceived ideas we have about life?'

'As I have said, the truth of life can only be understood by knowing yourself as an empty vessel, free from the ideologies of your tradition and society, religion and politics. How else can the true self be discovered?

If you look closely, you will see the pain you have constructed, the hurt you carry around, is also an illusion. If thought has created an image of who you are, being a false image, then you must also see it is this *image* which has been hurt. The pain is not real - because the image is not real. Can you see this, George?'

This was a little more difficult for him to take in, but he could see the reasoning behind it. He wanted to agree, but a feeling of apprehension raised itself into his mind. This *was* his reality, all he had ever known, and he couldn't dismiss it so quickly. 'Yes, I . . . . err . . . . understand what you say . . . . but it is difficult . . . . to just let go of . . . . '

'I understand your dilemma perfectly, and no-one would have any expectations of you to let go of your world. To release everything you have believed in to be real since your earliest days is never easy. But reality cannot be intellectual, it cannot be measured by what you experience because the experience is created according to what you *believe* is true. To know yourself is to look beyond what you have been told, without attachment, without prejudice and without conclusion. It is only when the mind is emptied of such falsities can the true self become apparent. But to do this, for most people, is such a difficult task.

So it has become a much slower process of evolution, a process of painstakingly letting go of the things which serve you no more. Of course it is easy to see within your society the progress man has made from a moral point of view. Society has always held an expectancy of goodness from the people living within that society, but again, for the most part, it falls down and never really progresses to acceptable levels due to the ugly state of its thinking.'

George was feeling a little more relaxed again and nestled back into the chair, knowing he wasn't expected to do anything.

'As we have discussed, the human mind is always seeking to be better, always looking for a way to break free from the pain it has put upon itself. You spend so much of your time thinking about this or planning to do that, all of which you hope will bring the security of a peaceful and happy state of mind. But the 'self' is separated and lonely, even though it tries to fill this void with as many pleasures as is possible, life still becomes a lonely existence from time to time, and, as the problems of life start to demand more and more attention, so too does this loneliness increase, bringing with it more and more fears that life will remain incomplete.

These are your circles of fear, George: fear of not having enough money, losing your possessions or your love relationships, fear of not being good enough, rejected by society as a loser, fear of the unthinkable happening to you and destroying your world. You are afraid of the future and condemned by the past, unable to accept 'what is' because you believe there should be more.'

This was exactly how life had become for George; a constant search for something to make him feel easier, something to stop him worrying, but his thoughts would never allow him to find it. 'Yes, I see what you mean, life can be very stressful.'

'It is indeed, when you are stuck in the middle of it, unable to see what is causing the problem. Many things in life are done with an instinct of belief it is the right thing to do, many things have been dealt with in such a way that may not be morally accepted by society, but, as we see, there is a blindness of thought, a madness of the mind that makes man quite unpredictable.

While ever man is living within his circles of fear, he easily attaches himself to a field of emotional pain which can make him act uncharacteristically. Fear breeds anger and revenge, envy and violent mood swings, fear fills a man's mind with jealousy and false images of society, until one day he cannot stand it any longer and reacts incomprehensibly against his outer world.

Again, if we take a look at the new generation growing up in this society, we can easily see how difficult it becomes to live within the pressures applied to them these days. What about your own children, George? I am sure you have experienced many mistakes they made whilst growing up. Mistakes which led them towards actions which were not acceptable to you or Phoebe. Actions which were quickly corrected and recognised as completely out of character for them.'

He remembered Neville had been suspended from school on one occasion for fighting . . . . this was something they would never have expected . . . . and Sonia went through a phase of telling lies to protect herself from criticism. 'Yes, this is true . . . . but my children's mistakes were extremely minor compared with some crimes I could mention.'

'Indeed they were. Your children were naturally evolving, making mistakes and learning, and all the while you accepted this and helped them move on, because the love you have for them allowed you to look beyond their mistakes to the true souls they are, but with the same understanding it could be said you would forgive much more.'

Shuffling nervously, George defensively crossed his arms. 'Well that would take some thinking about.' He considered the severity of some of the crimes shown on the news which were unforgivable in his eyes. It seemed to him society was getting worse, not better.

'You see, the world is waiting for forgiveness. Man in his ignorance and confused state of mind is waiting to find freedom from the temporary insanity of his mental consciousness. He is looking for release from the circles of his fear constantly tugging at his thoughts, pulling them into the dark side of his mind.'

'But I can't forgive the actions of a madman. Sometimes the most grotesque crimes are committed and, well . . . . I'm sorry, I can't forgive them.' He took a deep breath, starting to feel quite irritated.

'Maybe that is because you are trying to forgive the action itself, George. As I have said, forgiveness looks beyond this and recognises it was something the true self would never do. It does not condone the madness of insane action in any way, but feels a compassion for the twisted mind which sadly has been able to behave in such a way.'

'But what about people who murder or violently hurt other people? What about the families of victims? How could they forgive when they have lost so much . . . . ?'

'The pain of losing a loved one is a great cross to bear, something which takes unbelievable strength to overcome. Murder and violence have to be eradicated from your world - this is without question - but while ever the mind is fuelled with symptoms of such behaviour, then it will continue. While ever the mind gives justification for conflict on a collective level, it will also continue on an individual basis.

The act of violence is a consequence of irrational thinking by confused minds which have been programmed to respond in such a way . . . . your graveyards of war would tell you this is so.

There are some very famous words written in your world which unfortunately have been misunderstood by many: 'Forgive them, for they know not what they do' . . . . perhaps you will try to better understand them now.'

A calmer feeling came over George as he contemplated the words spoken, his emotions felt lighter and his body less tense. He started to realise the severity of the problem, the human mind had certainly become lost into a strange world of unpredictable behaviour, he could see this now and knew something had to be done . . . . but what, he didn't know.

'When you can understand the true reality of life is hidden behind a world of thought, behind a conditioned, prejudiced mind, when you can discover the love resting beneath your circles of fear, then you can teach your children well, you can show the world there is another way to live.

Forgive yourself and forgive your brother, for, in truth, you are not separated by anything but your own thoughts. The reality of life is guided by the fact that you are one and the same energy. You are all the same: evolving, conscious energy of love.

Let your children see this, with clear understanding, and let them be who they are' . . . .

✳ ✳ ✳ ✳ ✳

'Without love I am orphan to the streets of life,
my heart is closed, my hands are tied,
my dreams are lost, my path is gone,
my throat is weak without a song,
my mind is longing to be free,
for only love can love but see.'

Adam Katowycz rested his back against the newsagent's red brick wall, sheltering under the blue and yellow canopy which protected him from the persistent drizzle falling down from the heavy grey clouds. He opened his new packet of cigarettes and screwed up the cellophane into a ball, flicking it between finger and thumb as far away as possible. Taking one out, he placed it between dry lips, his eyes surveying the leaden sky. It was rough . . . . but it was good for him . . . . good for what he wanted to do. The light was dim and he wouldn't be seen too clearly and the rain was making everyone rush about with heads down, concerned with their own business.

Lighting up the cigarette, he nervously exhaled the smoke from deep within his lungs. He had thought through very clearly what he would do, and for reassurance, his hand reached deep inside his hooded jacket to touch the cold tip of the small screwdriver he had taken from his father's old toolbox in the garden shed. He caught sight of his reflection in the newsagent's window, revealing his hair now flattened from the weight of his hood and took time to carefully lift it up again, all the while drawing energy from the nervous intensity building up inside. He allowed himself an uneasy smile of satisfaction and returned his attention to his strategy.

First of all he would disable the car alarm. That was important. He had the screwdriver to gain entry . . . . he had seen the easy way to open a car door on a computer game. Then, when he was inside, he would start up the engine . . . . he had seen several of his mates do it before without a key . . . . and the car would be his.

Finishing his cigarette, he screwed it purposefully into the ground with his shoe, pulling his hood back over his head, it was imperative for him now not to be recognisable through any surveillance cameras. The car park he had chosen was behind 'Betta Value', a small supermarket on the extremity of the shopping centre with a quick exit away from town.

He whistled softly as he made his way down Wadsworth Road, branching off to his left past the Natwest Bank and along the pedestrian footpath up towards the car park. With every step he could feel the rush of adrenalin pumping through his veins and he marched on excitedly, occasionally lifting his head to check for security cameras. He could see two staring down at him, set high on their grey metal posts, like giant giraffes surveying the terrain . . . . he would have to take a chance, but with his hood up and his head kept low, he should be safe.

Finally arriving at his chosen site, he lit another cigarette and scanned the car park. It wasn't too busy this morning with maybe fifteen or twenty cars parked near to the building as people didn't want to have to walk too far in the rain. But Adam was patient, he would wait for one parked nearer the edge, where it was unlikely he would be disturbed.

He positioned himself under the flat perspex roof between the rear entrance and a huge pile of empty cardboard boxes by the loading bay and drew on his cigarette. The timing of his move would have to be perfect. Once he had targeted a suitable vehicle, he figured he would have at least ten minutes to complete his task before the owner would come back out of the supermarket, by which time he would be long gone. He considered the cameras again, and tugged at his hood, breathing deeply to clear the smoke from his lungs.

Soon his adrenalin lifted to a new high as his eyes fixed on a red Vauxhall Astra slowly turning into the car park. Flicking away his cigarette, he willed it to stop in a favourable position and his heart began pounding as he felt again for the screwdriver. The young lady driver knew nothing of the consequences of parking in her chosen bay as she locked the car, raised her spotted umbrella and headed towards the entrance.

Now Adam had to be fast and remember his plan. He looked quickly around and advanced stealthily towards the red car. Taking a deep breath, he dropped his thin torso onto the wet tarmac between the front wheels, looking up into the engine to locate the alarm. Reaching high towards his right, he found it clamped on the side of the wing. His hands took hold of the two wires hanging together below the connection and pulling with all his strength, separated them from the mounting. He jumped to his feet again, his eyes darting around to check no-one was looking and lifting the screwdriver from his pocket, pushed it into the lock and twisted it sharply, hoping to release the catch - but the door held firm. He thumped it heavily with the palm of his hand and felt it move deeper inside the chrome plated fitting. Twisting it again, he heard the crisp 'clunk' of the mechanism as the door catch lifted. He opened the door and slid into the driver's seat, conscious now of his wet clothes, but they didn't matter, the alarm had not gone off and he was safely inside.

His heart beat vigorously as he took up the screwdriver again and prised open the steering control panel. He could see the ignition wires clearly, sitting neatly below the column. With the gearbox in neutral, he pulled the wires from the switch and twisted them together, making sure they were fully connected . . . . the engine fired . . . . and his heart pumped heavily against his chest as he realised there was now no turning back. His left foot searched for the clutch and he slid the car into first gear, glancing at the controls to locate the wipers as he lifted the hand-brake and moved slowly away, bucking as he tried to coordinate the change into second gear. He let out a big sigh of relief and settled behind the wheel as he accelerated carefully out of the car park.

Adam relaxed a little, blowing out a long breath as he checked the rear view mirror, knowing he was safely away. He focused his attention on his driving, shifting through the gears with more ease as he merged into the flow of traffic. He found the indicator arm and pushed it upwards, dropping down into second gear and swinging the car full circle around the Atlas Grove roundabout and headed back down Wadsworth Road away from town.

A great surge of pleasure filtered through his body and he began to smile as he looked at the car he had taken. It wasn't a bad choice, a few years' old perhaps, but he could feel the power of the engine as he pushed gently down on the accelerator. A quick glance at the fuel gauge told him it was half full, perfect for his little joy ride. He pulled the car into the centre of the road, indicating right and turning into the estate he knew so well. He lifted down his hood and ran his fingers through his hair, wishing his friends could see him now. He laughed out loud as he swung his new toy around corners, rallying between the parked cars, and then part way up the hill, close to home, he slammed on the brakes, suddenly remembering his mother would be in the area by now. Reversing quickly, he headed back down to the junction, turning left towards the shopping centre again.

He felt his pleasure heighten as excitement raced away with his thoughts. 'Yes . . . . yes . . . .', he spoke out, ' . . . . let's see what you can do.' He pushed his foot down and raised the engine into third gear, overtaking two slower cars as he sped towards the roundabout. 'This is easy!' His smile widened as he made his exit and lifted the motor through the gears again, pushing the speed up to fifty, glancing in the mirror to gloat at the cars he had left behind.

For a brief moment, Adam's pleasure dissolved into pain, as the hurt of his father's letter, and his mother's pathetic weakness flashed into his thoughts. He sucked in a deep breath, trying to release his anger, slowing down a little as he glanced ahead, his heart beating faster as the green light of the crossing changed to amber. Slamming the clutch down he dropped into third gear and pressed firmly on the accelerator. Fifty-five . . . . sixty. The quick burst of speed pinned him back into his seat, taking him a little by surprise, but it was just what he needed to lift his adrenalin higher . . . . high enough to leave his troubles behind.

In the blink of an eye he was at the tube station . . . . it was then he saw him. An older man with a briefcase, wrapped up tightly in an overcoat which looked a little too big for him. Adam had no choice. It was too late to stop. It was too late to slow down. He tried to swerve . . . . but it was over . . . . the sickening thud of metal against flesh . . . . the lifting up of the man's body as it twisted in the air and dropped heavily to rest without movement . . . . without a trace of life.

Adam froze as he stared long and hard into his rear view mirror . . . .
then sped off blindly into the drizzle . . . .

. . . . 'Forgiveness looks beyond the inept actions of the confused mind
and sees 'goodness' in everyone and in every place.' George sat forward
a little, intent on clearly hearing the voice's words. 'It does not cast out
or hold prejudice against different colour, creed or cultural heritage, in
fact, forgiveness rejects totally man's conditioned paralysis of the mind,
and seeks only the true oneness which is of each one and everything.

It earnestly looks upon the world as a changing place, constantly
reforming its ethical and institutionalized ways, as and when the time
is right for change. It rests in understanding and humility as man treads
carefully through his evolution, step by step, a little here and a little there.

Forgiveness knows man well and accepts his misgivings without
judgement, without condemnation, but with patience and true belief
that everything taking place is perfection, and that eventually the light
of man will shine brightly.

Forgiveness sees all life is on the same path, some a little further
advanced than others, but all journeying in the true direction.
Forgiveness is the result and understanding of everything we have
discussed, George, a barometer of peace from which you may release
your separateness.'

George was lifted by these strong, passionate words with a surge
of positive energy, and yet still doubted his potential to live by them.
'But there seems to be so much to learn, so much to remember, it is a
daunting task to me now.'

'Such a task is easily undertaken, George, with little effort. Once
you have allowed the higher consciousness of energy to flow freely from
the spiritual mind onto the old consciousness, you will find many things
will change very quickly and without sacrifice. Many of the old ways of
conditioned thinking will be looked upon as not wanted any more as
the new progressive thoughts, with finer energies, take their place.

Man has become a caged animal, wandering endlessly around his
confined space, always finding himself back where he started, but always

questioning why he cannot leave his prison. His defining ideologies do not stand the test of time as his mind progressively evolves, and so he exchanges the old dogmas for new philosophies in a desperate attempt to cultivate what he believes is 'right'. But when he has exhausted all his theories and reasoned with a thousand explanations for his shallow existence, he realises all he has done is to give things a new name.'

The voice was right, society was forever coming up with new ideas and ideologies with fashionable ways to live, but most of the time they were old, recycled ways brought to the surface again. George had seen them come and go over the years.

'It is the light of the spiritual mind which brings a shift in direction for man. He begins to see that his outward search for truth is to no avail and that the real meaning of life comes from within. Man is, at last, able to examine his beliefs more openly and lay aside his preconceived opinions and inherited tendencies.

Out of this new-found freedom man can now identify with all forms of life. He feels in touch with nature and a new sensitivity rises in his heart. He acknowledges the violence of the world and the envy and greed of society. He sees the vanity and mindless self-centred actions of man, he touches the pain of the civilised world and knows that all he feels, all he sees, is written deep within his own make up. He recognises it is there through his own heritage . . . . but now a new, higher consciousness, taken from a foundation of love and peace, has allowed him to rise above it, and yet he may still show compassion for those who still have need of it.'

The voice was pulling George along now with a buzz of excitement. He felt good, here in this Library, now slowly starting to believe there was more could be taken from life. 'So this new consciousness is waiting for me beneath my conditioned behaviour?' He lifted his arms, clasping his hands together behind his head.

'Yes, it is there for everyone. Let us look at the human mind from this point of view. There is a light of the true self at the centre of your being, a light which is patiently waiting to shine through onto everything you do. At the moment, this light is blocked out, shrouded by misunderstood teachings, masked by unreasonable suggestions poured into the mind from birth, blanked by the likes and dislikes, hurts and circles of fear you have collected freely along the way, but as you start to look beyond these layers of obstruction, you will find the light will shine more and more. It is like peeling away at the layers of an onion, slowly taking away each one until you are left with the core - the light of the true self.'

Unclasping his fingers, George stretched his arms out wide, his mind steadied by the simplicity of the conversation. He stood and wandered around the table thinking of all the times he had felt under stress, forever complaining. He recalled the darker moments when he had felt so bad he had not been able to speak to anyone and life just seemed to crush everything he believed in. But here he was, gaining confidence, able to see there was something beyond the pain and loneliness of life, something which was his by right. He took a deep breath, as if filling his lungs to release all his problems, and slowly walked back to the chair.

'You see, George, the confusion you feel can never be *turned into* clarity and wisdom. Confusion must be observed very closely to see what is creating it. Each layer of obstruction has to be looked at directly and released, allowing lighter energies to take its place, until you are closer and closer to the core of your being. When you have released your violence - you will be peace. When your suffering is gone - you will be joy. When your pain is lifted - you will be love. It is all very simple and logical, even to the intellectual mind.'

'So to understand and release the old consciousness . . . . will enable the new consciousness to take its place?'

'As I have said, George, to be attentive and understand the great deceit of the mind, is enough to release the burden of it. Challenge yourself to find this understanding - and you will see it is possible.'

George moistened his lips and stretched his neck, rotating it from side to side, his thoughts focused deeply on this new revelation.

'There is a greater truth inside you, urging you to be more than you already are, but firstly, to progress, you must be able to see 'what you are not'. When you have raised yourselves above the violence and class differences, beyond the snobbish, self-centred attitudes with their endless pursuit of material wealth, when your mind is no longer projecting itself into the future, wishing for something to expand its conceited outlook . . . . then you may find this truth.

It is not something you can find externally. It is a movement from inside which will rise and fill the space you have left for it, and when it comes . . . . you will certainly know.' . . . .

. . . . With heavy breath, Adam Katowycz thumped his fists onto the steering wheel of the red Astra car. His heart thundered as he swiftly checked in all directions to make sure no-one had followed him. Fumbling around in the side compartment of the driver's door, he grabbed a dirty yellow duster and frantically rubbed the gear stick, handbrake and steering column. He dropped it to the floor and, looking around again, pulled his hood tightly over his head.

Adam knew it wasn't his fault, he had done everything possible to avoid the collision, swerving the best he could to avoid him . . . . but the stupid old fool had just walked out into the road without looking. He took a deep breath and jumped nimbly out of the car, shuddering as he looked back at the dent in the front wing and cleared his throat of mucus, spitting it out onto the floor as he walked slowly away as nonchalantly as his adrenaline would allow.

Adam tried hard to pull his confused thoughts together. Where would he go now? What could he do to escape this disaster? Should he go home . . . . hide in his room for a while . . . . pretend he had been there all day? They would never know it was him who had driven the car, how could they . . . . no-one had seen him take it? But his mother would be there . . . . she would ask him where he had been. To the shops, for cigarettes, he would tell her. If only the old man had looked . . . . none of this would have happened.

He marched on with head down, back towards Wadsworth Road. In the distance he could make out the Natwest tower peering down over the wet slate roofs, and wondered if he should go straight home now, or walk back, past the accident, as if he had never been there? He questioned his plan. Maybe the man was alright . . . . maybe he had taken a knock and then got up and walked away. That would mean there would be nothing for him to worry about, he could just carry on with his life. Surely it would be better for him to know the outcome of the accident, one way or the other.

He thought about it for a moment and decided to walk back, to face his fear, before he went home. He reached inside his hooded jacket and pulled out a cigarette without removing the packet, and for a moment his heart faltered as he punched his pockets to find the screwdriver, praying he hadn't left it in the car, but his fears were released as the short stub of the handle pressed firmly into his chest. He spat again and fumbled around to retrieve his box of matches.

Lighting the cigarette, Adam inhaled the smoke as his vision fell again towards Wadsworth Road. He could see the traffic, bumper to bumper, inching its way carefully towards the tube station. Suddenly he froze to the spot, his heart beating faster, leaving a sickening feeling in his stomach.

In the distance there was an ambulance with flashing blue lights eerily spreading through the fine drizzle onto the scene of his fearful sight. He could see people gathered round in a huddle, he gulped and tried to fill his lungs to overcome the grip of anxiety disturbing his body and tried to raise himself above the heads of the crowd, then shrank down again as he heard the piercing sound of the siren shrieking high above the dull drone of the traffic and idle chatter. He drew deeply on the cigarette and put his head down, fearing the worst.

He turned away, dropping his cigarette, a numbness filling his being like a shroud of loneliness he had never felt before, like a void of emptiness he was unable to fill with anything of meaning, anything that would ease the pain of his anxious cry for help.

Adam sidled away as the onlookers dispersed, walking slowly at first, and then fast, faster than he had ever walked before, away from the tube station and shops. He strode on, not looking at anything, not hearing the groan of traffic picking up speed again, not feeling the wind gusting at his face, not thinking a single thought to ease his despair. On and on he strode, far beyond the tree-planted verges of Wadsworth Road . . . . and then suddenly, with an instinctive pull, he stopped and looked around, suddenly he knew he had to go home, he had to go to his room, he had to go somewhere he could think straight.

He lit another cigarette and turned around, walking back towards his mother's house. No-one could blame him for this, it wasn't his fault . . . . surely it wasn't his fault . . . .

. . . .'But how will I know? How will I know when this new consciousness has risen?'

'You will feel it in your heart, George, it will be a light burst of energy which you may feel as love or happiness, with a greater awareness of what is happening around you. You may suddenly feel as if your problems have lifted away and that the road ahead is a much more pleasant walk than you imagined. It is a peaceful feeling of somehow knowing that everything is perfect and there is no reason for you to be anxious or worry about anything at all, in fact, it becomes clear to see that everything you did worry about was just an illusion of your thoughts taking your mind into a darker place.

It is a treasure trove of true creative energy, with a vast openness of understanding and compassion for the human race. But my words are only superficial, it is the experience which will bring a better knowing of this heightened state.'

'So this new consciousness will change many things.'

'As more and more people feel the lighter impulses from the spiritual mind, many of the 'old ways' will be gone as the world will undergo a 'peaceful revolution'. Man will no longer be content to enjoy luxury while another man starves. He will not be able to oppress and exploit his fellow man for monetary or political gain. Barriers will be broken down between countries, between sects and religions as man realises they were just fragmented ideas of the old system of thought.

Education will change giving children equality of learning, promoting the unique skills they have to create a new society of togetherness, a society which has given up its 'dog eat dog' attitude and is more able to help each other enjoy the goodness of life.

Once man has experienced this new consciousness, he will feel uneasy, and look around with a feeling of discomfort at the sight of suffering. The old self-centre of separateness will start to fall away and it will become more and more painful to sit back and watch the pain of others, consequently a much greater effort will be made to help relieve it.

There is a much better, more evolved world ahead, George, and you will be a big part of this world.'

'But I can already see a lot of these things starting to happen. People will no longer stand for being bullied any more. There are action groups set up to change many situations which we no longer want to see, many people are speaking out against wars and political regimes.'

'It is the start of the 'new age of man', the opening up to the new energies of a better world. The tide of change is just beginning to be felt, and as it grows, will sweep away all that man has built falsely, laying a foundation for better things that will be of a lasting nature, but the change will not come through violence and war, hatred and revenge, it will not be made through greed and selfishness or political strategy.

You see, George, the world you have now is an intellectual creation, a creation brought about by thought and past experience, pushed together by mechanical means and held firmly bound by threads of fear you have woven in between the fabric of life. It is not enough for man to continue walking his path with unworthy motives, creating disaster after disaster, conflict after conflict.

The wind of change is from a different direction, beyond egoic, intellectual values, beyond the circles of fear which you cling to so dearly. It comes as the result of a great and growing love, promoting a deep feeling of kinship between all men.'

George couldn't hide the excitement feeding the vision he was holding of a new world. He thought of Phoebe and smiled broadly as he imagined himself sitting her down and telling her of things to come, as if he were some sort of guru who could look into the future. He bit on his bottom lip and his eyes glistened in the natural light falling across the Library as the voice pulled back his attention.

'First of all, there is a time of preparation, a time of understanding that all this is going to happen - but it is a continuing process and will not happen immediately. Once the lighter energies of the spiritual mind have touched the conscious mind, there is an unfolding of the darker side of man, a release from the pain and hurt he has placed himself into. He finds a 'higher self' which helps him to take stock of 'what he used to be', yet now allows him to be a much kinder individual, with an openness and honesty which stretches with a vision of freedom out into the world.

But man cannot recognise this freedom, man cannot see beyond his individual status until his new found passion is ignited with the understanding that many men of the world still have not been able to lift themselves beyond the pain and fears of their unstable minds. There are still many unsavoury acts of violent, bad and inappropriate behaviour which are extremely undesirable to the awakened mind, and yet, can be seen as acts of madness perpetrated by a mind which has been conditioned in madness.

The awakened mind can now see that society has given man a dual personality with an intelligence to move in either direction. On the one side he seeks goodness and security of love with a peaceful nature, whilst on the other side he is the vengeful, wounded animal of pain. It is the awakened mind that recognises man's insanity, yet knows it is a temporary state of blindness. It is the awakened man who recognises the plight of his brother, and with compassion and true understanding, can forgive his madness.' . . . .

. . . . Wearily removing her nylon overall, Catherine Katowycz folded it neatly and shoved it back into her canvas bag for the following day. It had taken her nearly fifteen minutes to wash up and she had already done enough cleaning at work to make her disgruntled with the extra load.

She was sure she had left a note for Adam, asking if *he* would do it . . . . but he hadn't. It wouldn't have been so bad if the dishes were hers, but they were mostly his, left dirty with dried-on food and dumped into the sink. Wasn't he old enough now to show some responsibility around the house? She was too soft with him, too easy-going . . . . that was the problem. She would talk to him about it, but for now, she just wanted to put her feet up and rest for a while. She surveyed the shiny pile of pans, plates and mugs and decided to leave them to drain.

Where was he, anyway? He never seemed to be at home any more. She wondered what he got up to when he was out and shook her head despairingly as she made her way into the lounge, slumping down into her favourite chair. She picked up the television remote control, pressed the 'on' button and sat back to relax.

It seemed the television was all she ever had in life now. She never went out any more, only to work or shop, she never had visitors . . . . just hours and hours of constant television programmes. Sometimes she would find herself just staring at the screen, not even watching the programme, as if in some sort of trance, her thoughts far away, tied to the past . . . . or dreaming of better things to come in the future.

She would spend hours remembering the young girl she used to be, happy with life, making the most of her childhood, and then falling in love and starting a family. It all seemed to be so easy then, with Yvan by her side. But then, everything changed so quickly . . . . in the blink of an eye it was gone . . . . and she was here, alone.

What could she do? She had to do something to change all this . . . . but what? She didn't know any more. The more she sat and thought about it, the more pressure there seemed to be. Sometimes it felt as though she was weighed down with too many problems, each one pulling at her, making her afraid, even of her own thoughts.

She closed her eyes and tried to rest. The television set droned on, almost hypnotically allowing her to relax, pulling her away from the turmoil of her world.

Eventually she opened her eyes and quickly jumped up from the chair. What about Adam? Where was he now? She started to worry again and walked over to the window, pulling aside the net curtain and peered out through the misty rain. The weather was no better now than it had been all morning. She looked out to the dark skies with a longing for summer again.

Glancing down the street, she could just make out a lonely figure walking quickly up the hill towards her house. It was Adam! He was coming home. She watched him walking, her heart rising with love for her boy . . . . her life. He looked up as he reached the gate and she smiled through the window, but he didn't see her.

Catherine waited a moment after the door slammed, but there was no greeting or recognisable sound of communication from him. 'Adam?'

she called out, making her way into the hallway, but he was already hastily climbing the stairs. 'Are you alright, son . . . . do you want something to eat?' She tensed up a little, sensing things were not well.

'No, just leave me alone.' Adam's reply was abrupt. 'I just want to be left alone.' He hurried across the landing to his room. She could hear his door slam, the sound she had heard a hundred times, the rejection wrenching through her body, jolting her love into a chasm of pain.

Catherine wandered slowly back into the lounge and dropped down into her chair, staring hopelessly at the television. She swallowed hard . . . . but today she couldn't stop the tears swelling in her eyes . . . .

. . . . Pushing back his hood, Adam quickly removed his jacket and tossed it down to the floor. His breath came in short, sharp bursts, his stomach still twisting and turning in tense anxiety as he kicked off his shoes and crashed onto his bed. He sat huddled tightly, staring at the wall, trying to blank out the happenings of his day, pushing them away from his thoughts, telling himself it didn't matter, everything would be alright. But a voice from deep within told him it *did* matter. He should never have taken the car in the first place . . . . it was wrong to steal and he had been driving too fast, carelessly breaking the speed limit . . . . if he had driven slower the accident could have been avoided.

Guilt swirled around like a knife stabbing at his heart; a disconcerting presence which wouldn't leave him alone. He argued back. It was only a bit of fun; it was the man's fault; it was he who had stepped into the road, anybody would have hit him. But the knife twisted again with a sickening wrench to his stomach, leaving his torso to consume the pain of his actions.

He stared hopelessly out of the rain splattered window, breathing deeper, trying desperately to preserve his confidence, helplessly searching for something to believe in, a glimmer of hope that would make him feel better. He wanted to shout out aloud 'Help me . . . . I didn't mean to do it, it was just something to do, it was a game . . . . only a stupid game.' He put his hands over his face, feeling the cold beads of perspiration filling his forehead . . . . and then the hot tears.

The moist swelling of his eyes, at first slowly, then uncontrollable sobbing of relief, as though his heart had burst, releasing every emotion he had ever felt. He was angry, and then he was sad, strong, then helpless. Inside, a river of tears tore into his being, retrieving the very essence of his deepest fears. He was a man filled with hatred and unrest - and then, suddenly, a child again, with arms held out wide, reaching upward, grasping high into the sky, searching with longing for an answer to his pain.

Adam lifted his shirt and wiped away at his tears, his heart slowing a little. His breathing steadied and his head began to clear as he gazed around the room with swollen eyes, the posters on the walls glaring at him, enticing his thoughts to return back into his own mad world, a world he had made all for himself, a world he couldn't seem to understand any more. He wanted to run away and hide, he wanted to leave it for ever and never return. He wanted more from life . . . . surely there was more to life than this?

He gazed out of the window again, beyond the twisted thoughts of his mixed up mind. He craved the peace he could never find in a world he despised. He wanted to laugh and be happy, to find something to ease the pain of his cold crucifixion. He wanted his mother, he wanted his father . . . . he wanted someone to love . . . . but he didn't know how.

NO FEAR

'Am I not amazed by my own powers of intuition?
For behold, inside me I have found a weaker self,
and within its very nature, does it speak to me of weakness.'

. . . . 'And so you may see that man is ready to move on, ready to evolve beyond the heaviness of his mixed up state of mind. Moreover, it is evident that if he does not, then it is possible that his inner torment will lead him to the destruction of his 'self' and also of his outer world.'

George looked up into the open spaces above his head, the shock of the accident with his abrupt awakening in this vast room of books had eventually been dispelled by the voice, the strange visions and childhood memories he had tussled with had gone now. He was alive when he thought himself dead, more open to life in many ways and filled with an excitement of anticipation for what would happen next.

Phoebe would just love all this, to her it would be a dream come true, a chance to examine her spiritual knowledge. It was different for him, he had no spiritual aspirations in the first place, far from it. But now he could see there was much more to life than he had ever imagined and how important it was to open up to the spiritual mind. He coughed and cleared his throat. 'Go ahead, I'm listening.'

'We have already discussed how this evolution to a new higher consciousness will come about; the spiritual mind is ready and waiting to be touched upon, ready to shine the light of the true person you are

. . . . but is blanked out by an incessant stream of irrational thoughts pinning you down into a pre-conceived idea of how life should be.

We have spoken of the psychological movement of thought, of time, and the fears that have grown within the mind encircling your thinking with too much pain, anxiety and stresses which are difficult to release, difficult to look beyond. But if we pay attention to these fears, if we can understand totally the cause of all this pain, then perhaps they can be 'let go of' and a new light of wisdom may enter your world.'

George was intrigued and rested his forearms on the table in expectation of more positive life analysis.

'As we have said, before the development of intellectual powers, man was very much like the animals, that is, he had an awareness or consciousness of his life condition, but this awareness was confined to matters external to himself. This 'physical consciousness', as we have called it, allowed him to live as the animals do, in a world governed by the physical senses and actions of the body. He was able to live his life in an almost instinctive manner, with knowledge of what was going on 'out there', but without the ability to think about it.

He could feel the physical sensations of touch, taste, smell, sight and hearing and recognise them as being pleasurable or painful, liked or disliked, but without his intellectual state, he did not know why he felt this way and was not able to pity himself or think about his personality, as would the man of today. In short, physical awareness alone allowed early man to 'know' of life, but he did not 'know that he knew'. Am I making this clear enough for you?'

'Yes, I err . . . . think I get the idea.'

'Let me put it this way. Early man could be likened to the horse you may see standing in the field every day in all kinds of adverse weather conditions. The horse knows it is an unpleasant thing to do and will feel the pain of circumstances, but, it doesn't know why it feels the pain. It doesn't look to reason its plight, or to blame anybody else for it, its consciousness is purely limited to external sensations.'

George nodded his understanding.

'So it becomes apparent that early man did not suffer from the psychological fears which have plagued his successor, and that with a physical consciousness only, man was never in more discomfort than that of the body. It is only when the new, mental intelligence of man emerged did we start to see the beginnings of a totally new experience. Man had started to think about the way he lived.

The new man found he had risen above the intelligence of the animal, and could now do more and better things. He began to realise he had an active mind which allowed him to know himself better, as well as a growing understanding of his fellow man. He looked closely at the way he lived his instinctive life and made great changes to his lifestyle, taking away the pain and discomfort of his previous existence. He learned to communicate, firstly by signage, but then, as his 'mental consciousness' grew, through verbal sounds of the mouth, until eventually, a language was cultivated.

Tribes of men with different levels of intellect emerged giving rise to different cultures, different belief systems, and inevitably, differences of opinion. Intellectual debate and power struggles took hold, bringing with them the first signs of argument and warfare. Battles of tribe against tribe, intellect against intellect, have since written the pages of history to a point where even to this day, there seems to be no end to man's conflict.'

Again, George nodded his understanding as the poignant image of the soldier flashed back into his mind, he shuddered a little, a tingle rushing down his spine as he remembered his clear vision of war. He tried to relax again, blowing out a deep breath and shifting his thoughts back to the calm, peace of the Library.

'All of this and much, much more has happened to the world since man started to open his mind to new horizons and to think about what he was doing. But with the expansion of intelligence has also come a darker side of living.

Man is physically frightened of the dark, of spiders, rodents and snakes, frightened of heights, fast running water and many other physical dangers, but psychologically he is fearful of life and what it may do to him. He has fear of not having enough, fear of losing, insecurities and doubts about himself and his future, fear from the past and fear of where he is going.

Man is burdened with the fears of his own society and culture, fears which are passed down from generation to generation, beliefs which leave him in a constant state of apprehension. This is the modern world you are born into George, a world where fear is now accepted as a way of life.'

George didn't realise the problem of fear was so bad, it wasn't something he had noticed too much in other people when he was worried about himself . . . . but he could sense it was all around . . . . and really just accepted as a way of life.

'The obvious physical fears of danger, to which there is an instant response, are fairly easy to comprehend. But the bigger problem for the human species is the fears of the mind, the psychological process of torment that everybody is aware of. This is the fear caused by remembering something painful which happened in the past and thinking it might happen again in the future, or simply by imagining the worst for your life situation: you may die tomorrow or lose the person you love most in the world, or your job may cease and take away the comfortable lifestyle to which you have become so accustomed. All these are your worst fears, twisting your mind with stresses and strain.

Fear is a fragmented image of disaster creeping into your world and crushing your dreams and aspirations one by one. Even before you have begun to realise them, they have been taken from you and shattered in the dim light of self-doubt. Every pleasure you have is turned into a never-ending barrage of pain as you seek to overcome the fearful insecurities of life - all of which are created by your own state of mind.'

The last few months had been the most stressful George could remember. He had had plenty of worries before, but managed to get over them in time, and maybe for a while he hadn't been too bad, but then it had started again, concerns about one thing after another. There didn't seem to be any real peace from it.

'But where are all these fears coming from?' the voice continued. 'Fear would have you believe there is nothing you can do to change your life, until life changes it for you. This is the deception which is buried deep into your belief system; you have been told that fear is to be accepted and covered up until your external world has become a little easier, a little less stressful, and *then* you may release it. You have been told that fear is beyond your control and there is nothing you can do about it.'

George knew from experience that this was true, this was how most people would deal with fear, by covering it up and trying to forget about it. 'It does seem ridiculous when you say it like that . . . . but what else can we do?'

'If you look around, anywhere within your outer world, you will not see fear in physical form, although if you become observant enough, there are many consequences of fearful behaviour, many responses to the fearful mind scattered in every direction for you to look at.

Fear is not an illness passed on from person to person, it is not a virus to be treated through medical attention. Fear is not something that may be seen and avoided and it is not isolated to groups of different people with certain ideals of belief.

So . . . . if it is not an external force waiting behind every corner to strike you down, then obviously, it is of internal origin, quite clearly it is activated and produced from within the mind.

You see, fear is a controllable internal force. This is the great secret that fear has kept hidden from you for thousands of years. The wonderful thing about this, George, is knowing that fear has no external controller and that *you* can be master of its every movement – this is the answer to your question.

Great strength can be taken from the fact that fear is an illusion of the mind that may easily be released. There is no credible reason for fear other than that which you have given to it. It has no substance of reality, no end result of physical capability, it is totally an idea of the mind, that without belief of thought, cannot exist at all . . . . this is what you must understand . . . .

. . . . It had taken Neville Eastwood an unusually long time to be served at the bar. He couldn't believe how many people were in the pub in the middle of the day; every nook and cranny seemed to be filled with little knots of work colleagues and friends, noisily munching their way through a hurried lunch.

He picked up the pint of beer, orange juice and little stainless steel flag in the shape of a number six and scanned the room for his sister. He caught sight of Sonia taking off her coat and placing it over the back of a chair in an alcove at the far end, which had just been vacated by a group of satisfied customers. Weaving his way over, he sat down next to her, pushing the orange juice in her direction. 'There you go, Son', he looked at her and smiled, 'haven't seen you for a while, how have you been?' Neville thought perhaps she looked a little thinner than usual, but, then again, she was never satisfied with the way she looked and made a point of trying every new diet thrown in her direction.

Sonia picked up the orange juice and gratefully took a long, slow drink, stalling for a short time before she answered. 'Oh, you know, not too bad. Could do with a holiday really . . . . just need to escape for a while.'

Neville reached out for his beer and held it towards one of the bright ceiling lights, checking the clarity and gave her a knowing sideways glance. 'It'll still be here when you get back,' he never really did have too much empathy for his sister, 'I suppose it's you and Pete and your new fella . . . . what's his name?'

Sonia sighed, running her finger down the condensation on the outside of her glass. 'It's Pete really who is making all the fuss. I've made my decision about him, so why can't he leave me alone?' She shot Neville a quick, disapproving look, 'and his name is Gary, by the way.'

'So . . . . are you and Gary living together now?' Neville questioned, pushing his free hand through his dark wavy hair in anticipation of quenching his thirst.

'Yes, he decided to move in with me a couple of weeks ago, but Pete can't accept it and is being awkward about the divorce, taking it to court and claiming more money for the house settlement than I can give him,' she took another long drink of orange juice, 'divorce is such a messy thing, it's as if money becomes compensation for hurt pride. I never thought Pete could be like that . . . . all I did was stop loving him.'

Neville disguised a smirk behind his beer glass. 'But you *did* have an affair behind his back,' Ever since they were children he had known how to wind her up and score points, and still enjoyed doing so, for some reason it made him feel in control.

'But Gary is special to me, and Pete . . . . well, we were going through a bad time. It's over for me and Pete . . . . and it's none of your business!' Sonia tossed her blonde ponytail, she had already risen to the bait.

'Ok, ok, I'm only kidding, but Pete is only asking for what he's entitled to, surely?'

'He knows I can't afford to give him the money he's asking for. He's just doing it to be nasty. He's doing it all for revenge. Anyway, I don't think I want to talk about it . . . . it upsets me too much.' She lifted her glass again, glancing around, hoping no-one was listening, but she had no need to worry, everyone had much more important things to say to each other.

'What about mum and dad, what have they had to say?' Neville lifted his beer to his lips and gulped steadily. 'Ahh, that's good,' he returned it to the table and turned again to look at his sister, 'I bet they are not too pleased.'

'It's none of their business either!' Sonia snapped. 'Okay . . . . Dad's been giving me a hard time . . . . but mum's been quite understanding, I think she knows how hard it is to live with a man who is so irritating.'

Neville laughed aloud. 'You can't say that about dad . . . . that's terrible.'

'It might be, but he's such hard work at times, you know that.'

'Hmmm, enough said on that subject.' They looked at each other and Neville felt sure he saw a faint smile trying to play on Sonia's lips.

'Two ham salad on granary for table six?' A waitress in a crisp black and white uniform appeared in front of them.

'Oh, yes, that'll be us.' Neville reached out and exchanged the sandwiches for the little stainless steel flag. 'Thanks, that's great.' He passed one over to Sonia and placed the other one on the table in front of him. 'I'm ready for this.' He winked at his sister, her piercing blue eyes holding his attention for a moment. He lifted the top slice of bread to inspect the contents and reached for the condiments from the little tray left by the waitress.

'Yes, it looks good.' Sonia allowed herself a little respite from the conversation. 'Thanks, Neville.' She turned her attention to lunch with contented animosity. She still felt resolute and would have to be careful not to let Neville push her too far with his sarcasm, he always had a way of bringing the worst out of her.

Taking a bite from her sandwich, she looked distastefully at the loudly patterned carpet matched with numerous differently patterned upholstered chairs, as is usual in the more modern public house, although some of the brass light fittings were more to her taste.

'Anyway, when am I going to meet Gary?' Neville's question jolted her thoughts and she turned back to him.

'You'll meet him on Sunday, if you are going to mum and dad's for lunch, I've already arranged with mum to bring him along too, and don't forget it's their thirtieth wedding anniversary . . . . today, actually.'

Neville groaned. 'Oh no, I'd completely forgotten. Maybe I'll ring mum later . . . . and get them a present to take on Sunday,' he reluctantly decided. He turned to face his sister, 'Does dad know Gary is invited?' he added, a touch of apprehension in his question.

'He will do by Sunday, and I've already told mum if he says too much, we will leave.' Sonia's face became set and her eyes hardened. 'It's my life . . . . and I won't have him interfering.' She took another huge bite from her sandwich.

Neville recognised the same stubbornness in Sonia he remembered from their childhood, a trait which made him feel uneasy, but nevertheless, decided to wind her up again. 'Well, you know what dad's like . . . . if he doesn't take to Gary, there'll be no compromise and things could get uncomfortable.'

'Leave it Neville!' She scowled back at him, 'I expect you to be polite as well. Anyway, there's nothing for dad to dislike about him.'

'Oh, don't worry about me, I'll be on my best behaviour . . . . it will be a good thing for me too, if dad is in a good mood.' Thoughtfully rubbing his unshaven chin, he added, 'you see, I'm hoping he will be able to help me out a little over the next few weeks.'

Sonia stopped eating to take a drink, her curiosity rising. 'What do you mean by that?'

'Well . . . . I told you I had plans for a new business venture with a couple of friends, setting up an architectural company and becoming self-employed . . . .' Sonia nodded with a vague recollection. '. . . . well, we have a few contacts that can help us bring some work in . . . . but I need some cash to start the ball rolling, and I was hoping dad would lend me the money . . . . a sort of short-term loan until we can get moving.'

Sonia almost spat out her orange juice. 'You can forget that idea, dad has been out of work himself for a long time, there's no way he will lend you money.'

'But it would only be for a few weeks . . . . until we started earning. Surely he has some money put aside for a rainy day.'

'Dad's rainy day doesn't include buying *you* an umbrella . . . . and anyway, you have always been so irresponsible with money, don't you think he knows that?' She recalled many times when he had borrowed money from *her* and never paid it back.

'But, I've changed, Son. I've grown up a lot now, and if dad can see this, then maybe he will help me . . . . that's what we have to do, tell him how much I've changed!'

'What do you mean . . . . *we?*'

'I, err . . . . was sort of hoping you would back me up a little . . . . you could explain to him the change you have noticed in me. He trusts you, you have always been his favourite . . . . his little girl, I . . . .'

'No, Neville. I will not lie to dad so you can deceive him out of money.'

'I wouldn't be deceiving him . . . . it's just a small loan until I get on my feet again.'

'I said no!' Sonia rebuffed his plea and turned away to finish the rest of her sandwich, wondering where she could purchase a similar brass light fitting.

'. . . . I don't suppose *you* have any spare money to lend me . . . . ?'

Sonia ignored her brother, lifted her glass to finish her orange juice and banged it back down on the table. 'Look, Neville, I have to go, I'm very busy at work and I've got enough on my mind without playing your little games.'

'But I was only thinking . . . .'

'I'll see you on Sunday, Neville, thanks for lunch.' She stood up and removed her coat from the back of the chair and throwing it around her shoulders, picked up her bag and walked away.

'But . . . . Sonia . . . . what have I said wrong?' But she was already at the door. Neville shrugged, and taking a big drink from his glass, continued with his ham salad . . . .

. . . . 'Fear is thought, George. Fear is the movement of thought in time. It is not something life has thrown at you, it is pure reaction to your thoughts about it.

Through thinking about what has happened yesterday, or what may happen tomorrow, you have built a permanent resistance to life. Fear of the known and fear of the unknown is a conscious arrangement of a thought system that can never accept what is happening now. Can you understand this? I want you to see this clearly before we move on - thought in time is the creator of fear.'

George considered the question carefully and could come to no other conclusion about this statement. Whenever he felt fear in his life, it was always because of his thoughts, always his thoughts drifting off and presenting him with fearful images. 'Yes, err . . . . I would agree with you.'

'Good, so it is through thinking about an incident, an experience, a state in which there has been a disturbance, danger, grief or pain that brings about fear. To see clearly that thought is responsible for so much pain and that fear is not an outside influence beyond your control is highly important in your quest to be free.

You see, most situations in life will, at some point or other, bring about a moment of fear, a state of mind which has become negative and therefore stressful for no apparent reason. Should we take a look at your most recent troubled time? The job interview that became so important to you and left your mind in such a distressed state?'

Again, his thoughts recalled the tension he had felt, hoping so much he would get the job and put an end to his money worries and . . . . help him find his self-esteem again. It had been difficult at his age to feel he could be rejected by society. 'Okay . . . . if you think we should.' He spoke nervously, wondering what the voice would say next.

'Can we say, perhaps, your thinking, prior to the interview, was shaped by many different factors, each one bringing with it its own fearful outcome? Firstly, from a financial point of view, it was necessary for you to start earning money again. Over the years it had been comforting to know you had enough and, of course, it is easy to become accustomed to a good lifestyle.

But, moreover, your thoughts were driven mainly from a personal quest to be recognised and wanted again by a society which is quick to close the door on anything less than what it believes to be competent. You have in your mind many achievements from the past, and quite rightly are proud of who you are and all you have to offer, not only in a working environment but also within the personal relationships of life.'

Nodding his head, George was intensely interested with the analysis he was hearing. It was true he wanted to be respected as a man; a good man who would always do the best he could.

'It is easier when you are younger to take the knocks of life and bounce back with a confidence that you will overcome the setbacks befallen you, but as you get older, the fears of rejection become more and more hurtful as society proclaims 'it is a young man's world'. And so it is quite predictable that your thoughts have conjured up such images of rejection, disappointment and perhaps a feeling of worthlessness. These are the very images society would have you believe are now yours to battle against.'

'But this is just how it is in today's world.'

'Yes, we have already discussed how the psychological structure of society is based on comparison, competition, ambition and fear. It is written deeply into the mental consciousness of each individual to go out into the world and find security either through material gain and possessions or in personal relationship with other humans.

Consequently, man has built his empire and given himself every available piece of modern day living in the hope of finding total fulfilment, but as soon as he fills one space with the illusion of happiness, another one opens with the inevitable fear of his certain demise. Man is invariably torn between his pursuit of happy days and the pain he finds himself in when he cannot have them. He is surrounded by society's 'problems' and blinded by ineffective solutions which prevent him from finding any form of stability.'

George knew this was true, life appeared to be a constant battle to find something that would eventually bring a permanent state of satisfaction . . . . but he had never been able to find it. The voice was right, there was no stability in the society he lived in, it was always changing, leaving doubts in his mind about the way forward. 'But I suppose this is because of the fears we have . . . . I seem to be forever fighting against something and never getting on top of it.' He took a deep breath and blew it out in frustration.

'You see, this is constantly happening in your mind, destroying everything you hold as good. Negative, fear-based thoughts, conditioned by society, are taking away any chance of freedom you may have, and so you suppress your innermost feelings in the belief that one day they will go away.'

'But what else can we do . . . . we have to rid ourselves of them, don't we?'

'You will not rid yourself of fear by putting a lid on it. In effect, what you are doing is allowing it to simmer underneath the surface, increasing the power it has over you. This can only lead to further pain, and at the very least will release neurotic tendencies. Suppression is a form of intellectual explanation; you try to analyze your fear and give reason for its existence. You may say it is because of something that happened to you as a child, or it is because you do not have enough confidence. These, and others, are explanations you have given to yourself which allow you to accept and hold on to your fears. They do not help you to release them in any way, but reinforce the idea that you are a broken person, made faulty by events happening in your life.

Instead of looking deeply at your fear with the energy of attention to lift it from your being, you have decided it is easier to live with it and to give reason for its cause. Instead of releasing your insecurities and allowing a lasting understanding into your world, you have decided it is better to avoid the situations which compromise your thoughts and raise your tension.'

'But it is the only way we know how to deal with it.'

'It is indeed the way society has encouraged you to react, with its greedy, competitive nature pulling at your thoughts to overcome fear by the accumulation of power. But the more you accumulate, the greater is your fear of loss and the more insecure the mind becomes. Society has nothing to offer but a challenge of self-glorification with the pursuit of happiness its greatest illusion. For there is no happiness for the mind which destroys itself in the process of living. There is no peace for the mind which judges and condemns the weakness that is bred into every human being.

You may blame society and say something has got to change, but you are individually responsible for the way society is. Everything you see in your world is a reflection of everything inside you - it can never be anything else. Remember this when you demonstrate for change and if you really want to make a difference, try releasing something from inside which will have a direct effect.'

'What do you mean by that?'

'I mean, have you ever considered how society would change if the competitive nature of its existence was drastically altered? If, as individuals, you were allowed to develop from childhood to adulthood with a knowing that everything you did was a worthy contribution to a collective community? Wouldn't it be nice to consider that all life was an intrinsic part of a society which cared for everyone, young and old, with no judgement or condemning classification of background, intelligence, colour or social status?

Without competition there would be no greed or envy, ambition and deceit would be unnecessary. Without competition, fear of failure would not destroy the mind, which would be in acceptance of 'what is' and would not seek to find 'what it believes should be'. It would not be necessary to cultivate a centre of the 'self' and break away from the rest of humanity with selfish desires and false images of hurt and despair.

And we could go on, George, on and on with the changes that

would occur - all from the release of that one configuration of thought - 'competition'. Do you understand what I am saying . . . . the whole structure of society would alter significantly.'

'But that would take a lot of sorting out to change totally the way of society. It would mean a new outlook on life before it could happen.'

'That is exactly what I am saying. As individuals, it is now necessary to look at life differently. I am not suggesting society needs to experience an outer revolution, we have seen on many occasions how this type of change does not work. Many changes through violent revolution of outer belief systems have produced quite radical effects within society, but have systematically fallen back into bureaucratic order, the end result being that nothing really has changed.

Society is in need of a different kind of revolution, an inner revolution of sorts, where there is a reformed structure of self-belief, a 'letting go' of the authoritative conditions which have brought about so much pain and hardship. In short, if you were to look deeper into your being to replace the key factors of today's society; 'competition', 'ambition', 'wealth' and 'comparison' with a new order of action, to include; 'honesty', 'forgiveness', 'compassion', 'trust' and 'love', then you would be able to change your outer world.

While ever your mind is set into the 'old ways', you will continue along the road to disaster, but now is the time of change, now is the time to begin with a new system of thought. The challenge is there, laid before you, clearer now than it has ever been, and those who have eyes to see and ears to hear will step closer towards a new spiritual consciousness.

When you look at society, it can be seen that it tries desperately to bring about order within its own chaotic way, changing and organising, but it can never be assured of bringing peace to a conflicting world. The peace and order which you seek is not 'out there', but will come with a new psychological freedom, a new and deeper search for truth.'

George let out an exasperated sigh. 'This is getting frustrating for me now, I can see clearly what you are saying is true . . . . but still I am asking the question . . . . how is it possible for me, as an individual, to change society?'

'The truth is, George, it has been possible for you, as an individual to help cause the effect of the society you see before you now . . . . therefore it is surely possible for you, as an individual, to change the effect of that society.

For you, it means an investigation into your 'self' at the deepest of levels; it means you have to know who you are at the most fundamental part of your being and to question everything which has given you an identity.

At the moment you are blinded by the authoritative ways and beliefs society has implanted into your mind, into your thoughts. You have no freedom of self-expression beyond what you have been told is 'right' and 'wrong' . . . . but remember this, nationalism is a foundation for fearful thoughts, ideologies and religious dogma are the providers of unrest and separatist thinking. All such authority will bring about a state of mind which is in conflict with itself and the outer world and will only lead to chaos, violence and war.

At the present time, all of your fears are a product of a society which does not let you live beyond ideas and expectations of failure. You are cast into a die of limited capability because society itself is limited within a belief system of shallow thinking and confined action . . . . at the moment, this is the sad truth of your world' . . . .

'And so . . . .
Man did eat of the fruit from the tree of knowledge,
and a dark shadow did cast itself over his Eden.'

Sonia Richmond slung her bag across her shoulder and stepped out on to Wadsworth Road. Neville had not changed one bit. He was still living in a world of his own, always dreaming up smart ideas of how he was going to become rich and successful . . . . even using other people, whenever necessary, to get what he wanted. This time he was trying to take money from dad and she wouldn't be a part of it.

Hurriedly zipping up her coat and pulling over her hood, she weaved her way in and out of oncoming shoppers, her head bent low in the heavy drizzle, her eyes fixed on the wet pavement. She slowed her stride as she came level with Belvedere House on the opposite side, the place where she would sit and input facts and figures for the next four hours. She hated it, the monotonous routine of computer work bored her and the small, dark rooms with high ceilings and little natural light depressed her mood, but she did earn good money and needed as much as she could get at the moment.

Raising her head a little to take in her surroundings, she found the traffic still slowly grinding along, today almost at a standstill, making it easy for her to cross. She moved to the kerb edge, then hopped and swerved quickly between the frustrated drivers, glancing briefly towards the tube station where the trouble seemed to be. She shook her head, wondering what the cause of today's gridlock had been as she bounded smartly up the steps and through the polished wood of the revolving doors, unzipping her coat as she stepped into the entrance.

'Had a good lunch?' greeted the young receptionist, glancing up from her nailfile, as Sonia threw back her hood and wriggled out of her wet coat.

'No, not really.' Sonia smiled politely and made her way along the dim blue and grey corridor to the door originally marked 'Administration' in gold metallic lettering which now had obviously seen better days. She stepped over the threshold with a slight sinking feeling in her stomach and hung her coat and bag neatly on the metal-framed coatstand in the far corner and headed straight for the coffee, already made and left to keep hot in the glass pot of the filter machine. She had already decided she probably wouldn't do too much work this afternoon, after all, she had a lot on her mind; a lot she had to think about . . . . and it was strange how staring into a computer screen allowed one's thoughts to drift away.

She sighed a little as she poured her drink and clicked a sweetener into her floral bone china mug, stirring as she carried it back to her station. The other two girls who worked alongside her were still on their lunch-break, which made the dismal room seem even more depressing with its old-fashioned electric lighting and sash window at the far end not contributing much to the brightness.

She stood thoughtfully by her desk and took a sip from her mug, steering her thoughts back to Neville. If he would only take some time to think of anyone but himself, he would know mum and dad were stretched for cash, how could he even begin to think dad would lend him money? She coughed as the dark coffee aggravated her throat. Anyway, it certainly wasn't her problem and she would prefer not to get involved.

She sighed again, falling heavily onto her chair and composed herself ready for the work ahead. It would be a long day for her today, Gary would not be home until late and she would be lonely without him, but she didn't want to stop him having a drink with his friends, it was important to give each other some space.

This had been one of the problems with her and Pete, he had been too possessive, never wanting her to go anywhere without him, but still . . . . she couldn't help wondering what she would do all evening. Maybe she would take a long soak in a hot bath . . . . and paint her nails, she would pamper herself, and look forward to him coming home. Blowing her nose noisily, she discarded the tissue in the bin at the side of her desk and reached over for the top sheet in her 'in tray'.

There was a time when she and Pete had thought of having children, and she wanted to, sometimes desperately, but the time had never seemed right, there had always been other priorities. Now it was possible she would have to forget it; Gary had given her a hundred reasons why children were out of the question, and he was right; they had a long way to go as a couple, but she couldn't help feeling a little sad as she entered her password on to the screen and glanced at her input page.

Maybe she would end up a lonely old lady without having any children at all; nobody to help her when she needed it most. A great shiver of fear darkened her mind and she took another drink of coffee, spluttering again before pushing the mug to one side, there was nothing worse than luke-warm, bitter coffee. But Gary would be there for her when she was old; she had no need to worry . . . . they loved each other deeply, there was no doubt about that, and yet . . . . she could remember the day when she would have openly said the same thing about Pete.

Panicking a little she bent over her keyboard and started to press the keys. Maybe Gary would call or send a text to say he had cancelled his night out and would be home early. She stood up and marched over to her bag, maybe there was a message already. Fumbling deep inside the zipped pocket, she brought it into view . . . . but the phone was blank. She chewed her bottom lip and walked back to her computer, placing the phone on the desk next to her. How could she possibly concentrate on her work when her mind was filled with so many distractions?

Frowning at the keyboard, she tried to focus her mind on her work, but somehow her fingers were resisting the challenge, until eventually she gave up and sidled across the room to the window, gazing out to the overcast, grey skies, wondering where she would be in a year's time. Would she still be here, wishing her life away, inputting data which held no meaning for her, politely making conversation, pretending everything was alright, while all the time burning up inside? Surely the pain she was now feeling would go away. She was in love . . . . how could it be so painful . . . . how could it feel as if her world had fallen apart?

She stared out at the traffic, now moving again along Wadsworth Road, her confused thoughts drifting away. Her eyes followed the little groups of pedestrians milling around the pavement and wondered where they were going and if *they* all felt the same as her. She closed her eyes and inhaled deeply, trying to release her negative feelings, she shuddered and turned quickly back to the room as the office door opened.

'Hi Sonia, you won't believe what's just happened to me, I've just got to tell you! Are you alright?'

Sonia hesitated for a moment. 'Yes I'm fine.' She wandered slowly back to her chair. 'I was just . . . . well, I suppose I was just dreaming' . . . .

. . . . Staring down at the empty glass on the table, Neville Eastwood had a choice to make, either he could go back to his lonely flat and try once again to work out the projected costs of his business involvement, or stay and have another pint. He knew he couldn't really afford to continue drinking but the beer was good and his head was already a little fuzzy from the first one, so he decided upon the latter.

Picking up his glass, he steered his way carefully to the bar between the groups of chattering, lunchtime revellers, taking great care not to interrupt their flow of conversation or encroach upon their space, and waited patiently to catch the barman's attention. Eventually, he called out to him, 'That's a nice pint of beer, I think I'll have another one please,' he tugged at his ear, a habit he seemed to have acquired when not feeling too confident or talking to strangers.

Smiling, the barman turned to face him. 'Yes sir, was it a pint of Guardsman Ale?'

'Yes . . . . I think so.' Neville wasn't too sure, but reckoned the barman knew what he was doing. He watched him fill a fresh glass and dug deep into his jeans pocket to find the correct money, passed it over and shuffled precariously back to table six, making himself comfortable whilst waiting for his beer to clear.

He couldn't understand what was wrong with his sister. She had been edgy from the outset, obviously looking for something to fall out with him over, but he should be used to it by now, she had always been the same. He remembered from the earliest days, she had bossed him around and always made trouble for him with mum and dad.

He recalled a specific time when they were young. They had been boisterously running around, chasing each other, Sonia had knocked over and broken a favourite vase from the sideboard, smashing it into pieces . . . . and left him to take the blame. He had cried and pleaded his innocence for hours, telling the truth, but they wouldn't believe him. She was their golden girl and he had to make do with being second best.

As they grew older, his dad would criticise and condemn the way he did things, making him feel inadequate, telling him he should be more like his sister instead of acting the fool . . . . but he wasn't a fool, he could see what was going on around him, and he didn't like it much. He was so thankful he had managed to make university and escape their clutches for a while . . . . at least he had found some self-esteem again.

He raised his glass and took a long drink of beer. University had been kind to him in a way that stretched beyond just the educational side of things. For the first time in his life he had known the freedom of making his own decisions, without criticism, without having to listen to his father raving on at him. He had discovered other people *did* listen to him, approving his ideas, respecting his intelligence; he was a leader with inspirational thoughts . . . . Sonia had it wrong, he *had* changed, and he knew his plans were well thought out, it was just a matter of time before they came to fruition.

Neville considered himself a stable character with enough glowing charisma to reach the very pinnacle of society, and so it was with that vision firmly fixed into his mind, he settled his wiry frame comfortably into the scattered cushions of the alcove seating and lifted his glass, smiling broadly as he savoured the taste of the traditional dark-brown ale . . . .

. . . . Turning back to face her computer monitor, Sonia Richmond sighed, she had been listening, for what seemed like an eternity, to a verbal expression of events which meant nothing at all to her; a personal airing of grievances which were totally beyond her own range of understanding. She had blindly agreed with every minor detail of interpretation to a point where she could feel the anger of the situation herself. In many ways, she almost felt better for the sympathy and compassion given to her colleague. At least it had given her a little respite from the incessant thought forms of her own situation.

She shrugged her shoulders several times and rolled her head, tossing her ponytail from one side to the other, trying to release the build up of tension and began to hit the keys, focusing her attention onto the data in front of her, but her eyes were constantly drawn to the phone resting by the side of her cold mug of coffee. Reaching across the desk, she checked it yet again, but there was no message, no lifeline of hope to lift away her painful image of an evening alone.

There was nothing else for it, she took a deep breath and urged herself to be positive, after all, it was only one evening and she didn't really want to go out on a miserable Tuesday in November, but there were moments when her demons would rise up inside her making all sense of rationality disappear. These were the times she most wanted to be with Gary, she just needed to be loved, but when she looked at it with reasonable calm, she knew there was really nothing at all to feel anxious about.

She smiled to herself, feeling slightly better and turned back to the page of endless lists of facts and figures, allowing her concentration to rise as she skilfully moved her fingers across the keyboard, gliding instinctively towards the letters and numbers in front of her. As she fell into a trance-like state, her thoughts drifted back to Neville. Maybe she had gone overboard a little, walking out on him, she didn't see him too much these days, and he had bought her lunch obviously wanting to talk things over. She stopped typing and stared through the window, pursing her lips, for a moment she could feel the guilt of her selfish behaviour, but brushed it aside knowing Neville would sense it, too. Maybe she would text him to say sorry and started to reach out for her phone, but then decided to leave it for the moment. She would see him on Sunday and, anyway . . . . he would probably have moved on now to another scheming idea.

She sighed and turned back, hitting her keys with resignation . . . . at least it would pass the time . . . .

. . . . Neville Eastwood wriggled back into the little nest of cushions as he seated himself back down at his table and impatiently watched the cloudy mass of his third pint of beer settle.

He was frustrated with life; disappointed with the slow twists and turns that seemed to raise obstacles in his way, one after the other and stop him from reaching his goal. How slowly it took shape, when clearly he could see where he wanted to be, but how difficult to get there without setback. He didn't ask too much of life, only enough money to buy the things he wanted with enough time to enjoy them. He wanted a nice house and car, good holidays and someone 'special' to share them with. He wasn't greedy for vast amounts of everything . . . . he just wanted enough . . . . enough to be happy.

He glanced around the pub, the floor space was a little clearer now, the lunchtime rush was over for the black and white clad staff who were darting about picking up empty glasses and plates of half eaten sandwiches from the tables and the occasional screwed up serviette from the floor.

Neville looked at the people who remained behind, wondering if they had found what he was looking for. There was a group of suited businessmen gathered around the far end of the bar, enjoying a pint, some of them laughing, intent on light conversation. Others pulled up close together round a table, with briefcases open, discussing the affairs of the day. A couple of women, also in black tailored outfits, standing by the flashing fruit machine, sipping on their gin and tonics, something to do with the legal system, he thought. Over in the far corner an older man in an unfashionable denim suit and horn-rimmed glasses looked quite out of place, huddled up closely to a girl who must have been half his age, secretly whispering and clasping at each other's hands.

He could hear the buzz of music coming from another room somewhere behind him, and the muffled sounds of laughter, but he couldn't quite make out the words of the song, although he thought he recognised the tune and almost named it to himself, but gave up after several failed attempts.

He wondered what *he* must look like . . . . a solitary figure, alone with his thoughts, gazing about the room through alcohol-blurred eyes. He picked up his pint and enjoyed a long drink, a weird contentment starting to relax his muscles and ease his mind. He nestled deeper into his new found comfort and soon he was happy, without a care in the world; it didn't matter any more if he didn't get the money to finance his dream. It didn't matter because he didn't care. He was young and highly qualified with good ideas for the future, there was nothing could stop him from finding his pot of gold. He didn't care about Sonia and her stupid love triangle. He didn't care about his dad always putting him down . . . . he was happy to be exactly who he was.

He reached over for his beer, looking beyond his fears with an attitude of confidence. But as he rested back on his laurels, slowly, without warning, a nervous feeling of anxiety crept up on him and started to pull him back down.

Suddenly, his thoughts changed direction again. Of course . . . . he wanted it to work . . . . he had spent hours of his time working out figures with long-term projections to make *sure* it would work, and he also hoped Sonia would be fine, given time to sort herself out, she was his sister and he loved her.

He gazed around the pub with a questioning expression knotted across his brow. What was wrong with him? Why was he so erratic with his thoughts? He knew full well that alcohol was not good if he wanted to think straight, but why was he so angry, so confused? He took a deep breath, almost with a sigh of apprehension as he tried logically to analyse his strange behaviour.

Slowly he began to realise that his problem was more than the petty squabbles of families; more than his excuse to borrow money to finance a venture that any bank would consider . . . . it was a personal battle between father and son; a battle of acceptance, respect and love. It was a battle of the deepest need for him to win to reclaim his self-esteem and release him from the fears of his own inadequacy.

In one moment it could all be over, with a smile in the eye and a hug to the body . . . . and the words he wanted to hear ringing in his ears . . . . *'I am so proud of you son'* . . . .

. . . . 'You see, fear is a very complex issue to break down and analyse into any form of logical reason.' The voice's words echoed boldly across the Library. 'Fear is a reaction, a shock to the system which may be looked at for a thousand lifetimes to no avail, or dissected into the smallest of segments, still without a genuine conclusion of why or how.

There are so many different fears, so many reactions to every day occurrences that it becomes a never ending series of intellectual research to establish any form of pattern that may be broken to release yourself from the heaviness of your fears. But if you can once discover the cause of fear, then it becomes possible to let it go.

I am not talking here of the many different branches of individual fear that most people have, but of the root cause of all fears - this is where the problem begins.'

George could understand this philosophy. There were so many different fears that it would be extremely difficult to solve each one on an individual basis, but if you could go straight to the root cause of all fears . . . . perhaps then you could stop it.

'In any walk of life, everywhere you look where life is taking place, there is always a cause and, of course, the many effects of that cause. If you are walking down the street at a normal pace and suddenly start to run, your heart rate will speed up accordingly and your temperature will rise. These are the obvious effects of your actions, but to remove these effects, you have to remove the cause . . . . and so you slow down again.

It is quite logical to see that this is happening all the time and is an automated reaction in most cases. The effect of eating too much food or eating the wrong foods can easily be seen when you start to put weight on . . . . but, again, the normal reaction is to remove the cause and modify your diet accordingly.'

There was nothing too difficult for him to understand and he added his agreement. 'This is easy to see, it is common sense really.'

'Yes, for most occurrences in life it is quite easy to see that with a little common sense any such problem can be removed without too much fuss or anxiety, as I have said, it is all a matter of recognising the effect, and then removing the cause.'

George was curious as to where the conversation was going, but had learned to be patient and listen well.

' . . . . But this does not seem to be the way when it comes down to the action of fear . . . . for some reason fear is readily accepted as part of life, with an extremely painful outcome, the effects of which produce many undesirable illnesses of body and mind.

Your medical centres and dispensaries are full each day of people seeking to combat these mindful effects, but if you are physically ill, you would treat the cause of illness to alleviate the pain, so why is mental illness so different, why do many people take vast amounts of medicines to cover up their mental anguish? A pill is just another effect of the cause and will not make you better, yet it will dull your mind totally and actually prevent healing from taking place.'

It had only been a couple of months ago George had paid a visit to his doctor and had readily accepted anti-depressants to combat his stressful behaviour. He felt flustered now, here in this Library, knowing full well that the voice would know this . . . . but it was common practice, lots of people were doing it.

'The society you have created has decided that with any such problem it is wise and proper to treat the effects or condition and thereby is never able to remove it permanently.

Have you ever wondered why, with all the technologies you have in today's world, there is still a persistent problem of famine in various places? You are able to see the effects of such poor living conditions readily on your TV screens, but why do you not remove the cause of this terrible existence? Why do you insist on treating through ineffectual means? You see, George, with a little bit of consistent thought, many problems would be gone.'

There was nothing George could say to excuse this ridiculous mindset made so clear to him now. He had never thought of it in this way before, but once seen became obvious that it wasn't right.

'And so it is with the great problem of fear, a problem that is causing such great pain to each individual and within society as a whole. It is covered up and buried beneath a blanket of prescribed pills and many other forms of ineffectual escape, but the problem remains and will continue to do so until you are able to look directly at the cause.'

Again George could follow the reasoning behind this and pushed back his hair with a growing confidence.

'Now, we have already recognised the effects of fear and can see that they are a product of thought digging deep into the past to find something which it is fearful of and not wanting the experience repeated, or thought projecting fear into a future time bringing anxiety of what might occur.

So fear is thought in time, the inability of the mind to rest in the now and accept the present moment. This is the cause of all your mental anguish and consequently all the disturbing effects of such a mind. This is the obvious problem and the cause of so much pain. When you can understand this is happening, you may also see that you need to think differently.'

'But why does this happen? Why do we constantly search into the past and think of the future?'

'This is the world you have created for yourselves. Society has shown you many things, given you many reasons to relive the past and look towards the future'.

As children you are attacked by society, there is always the pressure, always the sense of being rewarded and punished. You are never able to be clear about who you are because there is this constant comparison between individuals, this constant competition to show who you can become. Consequently, as you grow up in such a society, the mind builds up a barrier of fear; fear of not being rewarded, fear of being a failure, fear of your own weakness being exposed and the people you love rejecting you. You are forever building on past failures trying to better yourselves.'

Casting his mind back to his own childhood, George could remember the pressure he had found himself under to do well and achieve high standards in his education. His parents expected great things from him, his teachers pushed him hard, he remembered the intensity of it all. But he also knew he had done the same with his own children, especially Neville, who had been rather lazy, he had pushed him all the way, but it was only now he could see perhaps it hadn't been the best thing to do.

'As an individual consciousness it is so difficult for you to break away from this trained way of thought and find anything new, anything of value, because politically you are groomed as a mass consciousness, you are educated to conform to a mass culture and tradition. You are persuaded that authority knows best for the people, and the people should accept political reasoning for their own security.

It is a systematic way of destroying freedom and rationalising any form of serious revolt. Life has become a robotic following of bureaucratic nonsense leading you along a road to ruin, and yet with a promise of fulfilment at the end of it. But when you can see this, when you can recognise the effects of this happening, then there is a responsive action from inside which tells you this is not right, this is not how it should be.

The same thing happens when you completely see and understand the cause of your fear. There is an intelligence which sees the illusion of thought and time and gives you a proper action to lift you away from your pain . . . . and with this action, there is freedom.'

Confidence continued to rise up inside George, with a strength that told him if he could do this, his troubles would be over. If he could just observe himself and the outer world very closely, he could see where his problems were coming from.

'Again, let me say, the human species has chosen to live by routines, habits and set patterns which, it believes, are the easiest and surest way to find security, but does not understand there is no security in a changing world - only disappointment and unrest. Man has learned to cope with his innermost feelings of despair by suppressing them, hiding them behind the false 'self' he has painstakingly adopted for himself and forever denies there could be any weakness at all to be ridiculed by his outer world.

Other people have turned to religion in the hope they can find something 'sacred' to relieve their pain, but in the end find out all they have done is shift their suffering from one belief system to another. It is impossible for thought to create anything which may be proved to be 'sacred', but thought has created many concepts of a divine reality which allows escape from the discomfort of the known.

All in all, following a religious ideal or to succumb to any mystical or evangelical dogma may bring short term relief to a conflicting mind, but in the long term will resurrect the old patterns of fear and may even strengthen their grip as they fall deeper into religious authority.'

This had never been something George could understand. He had always wanted to believe in some sort of higher order beyond the human way, but for some reason, religion had always seemed too contradictory, with so many different beliefs about the right way to live. He could now see, perhaps, there was a basic truth within all religions, and if this truth could remain consistent throughout, religions could unite and become credible within society.

'As each new generation grows, it is becoming more deeply embedded into a world it does not understand, and yet, quickly becomes accustomed to the mental consequences and tortures of such a world. Mental fatigue is setting in so quickly that the human machine is becoming dysfunctional and cannot cope with the demands placed upon it.

Everywhere you care to look, you will see the human race living in the fears of its own personal thoughts of helplessness and despair. Children are desperately reaching out for recognition in a world that places them deep within a culture of power struggles and dissociation with everything that is real.'

George nodded his understanding, 'Yes, I can see we are totally mixed up.'

'But we are not here to criticize the form of the human race, George, this is, and has been, the natural evolution of the species, through the physical consciousness of the animal behaviour to the development of mental consciousness and the expansion of intellect. This is 'where you are now', and you *will* move forward to the next stages of development. This you should not doubt.'

'You are very confident we will change.'

'Everyone should find good reason to be confident. We have already mentioned the changing path on which you walk, with higher, intuitive feelings of 'right' and 'wrong' moving you constantly forward. You may be puzzled with the details of 'morals' and 'ethics' and may not be able to understand fully the implications, but intuitively, you *know* the highest 'right' of which you are capable, and consequently, from this feeling, you are able to recognise when you have fallen back into the 'wrong' of the lower stages of your mentality. Through conscience you are able to correct yourselves.

This is a gentle process of evolution which cannot be ignored, and eventually, will carry you from your animal heritage to new levels of consciousness - the like of which you have long since forgotten.

The signs of mental unrest and discomfort are becoming more and more apparent as time goes by. The pain of life grows stronger as each generation tries to overcome the effects of living within a thought system that is depleted of new ideas.

Your political systems are failing because priority is placed on reshaping that which has already proved itself faulty. In essence, what you try to do is manipulate these failures instead of treating the cause. The education of children has become preparation for a working life which is filled with the fears of unobtainable goals and self-gratifying desires, consequently truth and honesty cannot prevail in a world which is clinging to the relics of a past consciousness.

But, the evolutionary process must continue, little by little, to show clearly 'who you are not' and to awaken within a new pattern of thought that will lead to 'who you truly are'. As the spiritual mind unfolds, the 'circles of fear' will be dissolved; one by one they will disappear, allowing the light of the new consciousness to take their place.

There are great times ahead for the human race, but it will not be through actions or promises of material gain - it will be through a change of thought.'

'But how can we think ourselves to change?'

'Through the spiritual mind will come impulses of truth; impulses of the one life that is given to all. There will be an understanding of the eternal presence of the light of your true nature which will change your perception and allow your fears to be gone. You will become closer to your fellow man as you perceive more and more the unity which is lifting you away from your old instinctive patterns. Values will change and societies will open up to allow a new wisdom of thought, leaving governments no other options but to change. Education will promote the new creative feelings of young people, expanding their consciousness with a greater self-belief. In every walk of life the new thought movement will bring people together of every colour and creed, every nation and culture. When gradually, all this is understood . . . . there will be peace upon the earth.'

'But what will bring this new thought?'

'It will come through an energy that has for many, many years been locked away inside you; an energy that has been lost behind many layers of your darkest fears, but as these fears are dissolved with the opening of the spiritual mind, it will rise eternally, filling the spaces you have created for it. To place your thoughts with this energy will be to change the face of everything you look upon, George, for it will grow and expand in a way you could never imagine. It is the true power of everything you are; the consciousness of the universe; the eternal light that will never die . . . . it is the energy of love.'

LOVE EACH OTHER

'And when I cannot say a word to hurt the world I see,
and when I cannot hear a sound to make me disagree,
when silence calls me home again and forgiveness sets me free,
the die is cast, my time is passed,
then love will be with me.'

'So . . . . what is love? This we have to find out and, contrary to what you may believe, George, it is not such an easy task.

In every walk of life everybody speaks of love, but do they really understand what love is? To most, love is the 'special relationship' between two people, the pledging of undying servitude and faithfulness allowing trust and honesty to keep those special moments alive. But is this love or just part of the search for comfort and security that man is everlastingly seeking?

If you look closely you will see that most relationships rely upon continuous emotional satisfaction, and when there is not, the relationship becomes tense and anxious, giving rise to anger and jealousy. Can the pain of resentment and jealousy be love, the same love which gave happiness and contented dependency at the beginning? This is a serious question, George.'

'I know what you mean, our relationships can be the strangest of things. One minute we are in love, the next we are not.' George filled his emotions with a great longing to see Phoebe, their relationship had been tough at times, but had survived the ups and downs and he had an overwhelming urge to just hold her in his arms.

'It seems that as long as you can rely on another to give you what you want, then you will love them, otherwise the relationship may turn sour, into what you call 'a love/hate situation', which becomes a very painful experience. But this is love to most people, a love which allows their desires and wantings to be fulfilled - or not, as the case may be.

Many people will say love is the pursuit of certain pleasures, be it sexual or self-gratifying in some form or another. Others love their work or love being part of organizations which offer them something different to extend their minds into. Nationalistic people say love your country and fight for the right to preserve the culture and tradition which may be under threat. But is this love, or is it just another form of escape from the painful fears of your mental consciousness? Has love become the name you have chosen as a conceptual idea which may help you in life to overcome your inadequacies?'

George was fascinated by this new love theory and could even see the truth behind it.

'You see, the concept of love has become a product of thought, it has become a manipulation of the mind, something to believe in which can make life better for a while. It has become fashionable to speak of love and endear yourselves to false images which in reality have nothing to do with love at all.

Love is not responsibility or duty. When you are compelled to act in a certain way or do favours for another out of loyalty, your actions are not based around love. Many parents responsibly prepare their children to have a secure position in society, but is this love or are they really more concerned with their own respectability and position? When you lose someone you love, do you cry for the person who has gone or for the loneliness you feel inside?

Do you live your life constantly seeking self-pity or can you find true compassion to reach out with? Are you free to love, to know and understand the quality and passion of true love? Do you even know what love is any more? All these, George, are questions you may ask yourself, but the answers you will find may not be such a comfort to you.

You will see that dependence is not love, jealousy is not love, you will find possessiveness and domination are not love, responsibility and duty are not love, self-pity and the never ending cycle of self-gratification are not love. All these are part of a process by which you believe you will find love, but they are just reactive measures in the battle to keep your fears under some form of control. The mental consciousness of man has developed a false love which is used as a weapon to fight against the stresses of life.'

'Are you saying we don't really know how to love?' George was a little astounded by this new speculation and wanted to get to the bottom of it.

'Everybody knows how to love, everybody can discover what real love is, but you will not feel the freedom and truth of it until you go beyond the movement of thought which has created its false identity.'

'But how can thoughts be powerful enough to change the meaning of love?'

'Thoughts are dynamic forms of energy, similar to light, heat and electricity. They have the power to lift your consciousness to the highest levels - but may also take you to the darkest places of fear. This would depend upon the vibrational energy of the thought. Of course, you already understand high vibrational, positive thought is uplifting, whilst the lower, negative forms are much more disturbing.'

'Yes, I can understand that . . . . '

'Every thought you hold and every action you take is based around one of two emotions - fear or love. In truth, there are only these two emotions and they stand at the opposite polarities of the world you live in. If you were to consider carefully, you would find everything created within your world is a derivative of either one or the other. This is how your human experience is created. It is why humans love, then destroy, then love again. Always there is the swing from one emotion to the other.'

'You are saying everything we do is some form of action between love and fear?' George wasn't so sure about this statement.

'While ever the mind uses psychological time to expand its thoughts from past to future, then it is true, those thoughts will either be rooted in love or fear. Now, as it is thought that creates action, then whatever you do in life is governed by these two emotions. Check yourself and you will see it is so.'

Running his hand over his hair in his habitual way, George tried to focus on his thoughts, whilst still trying to keep an ear on the conversation.

'The truth is you have been taught to live in fear. From your earliest years, the people you trusted the most, your mother and father, taught you love is conditional. They told you to be 'more of this' or 'less of that' and it is the 'survival of the fittest', the victory of the 'strongest' and the success of the 'cleverest' that will bring life's rewards. And so you strive to be all of these things, believing if you are something less, you will not be loved. You fear loss, because you have been told anything less is to lose.'

George stared down towards his feet, his thoughts now searching through his childhood looking to remember how he had felt in his younger days and was surprised to sense a twist of mixed emotions. There was always great love from his mother, but a touch of fear when he thought of his father and just for a moment he felt a little uneasy, but then realised his father was only doing what he thought was best for *him*.

'Having created a fear-based thought system about love, you then proceed to allow it to dominate your experiences. Not only do you see yourselves receiving love which is conditional, you also give it back in the same way. You take this conditional love into your relationships and expect each other to pamper the needs which will allow you to love. It is when these demands are unfulfilled that the relationship is said to have failed.'

'But I still believe relationships are built on love.' Again Phoebe instantly swept through his mind.

'Relationships are built upon a compromise of what you believe is love. It is actually a set of conditions by which you measure the 'specialness' between each other and so you are happy to trade whatever each one is offering. This is very pleasing for you at first and, of course, you have no doubt this is love, but after a while, as your needs start to change or become unsatisfied, so too love starts to fade, and with it your relationship. You see, George, conditional love is always a temporary state of mind. It is a result of a thought system which is based upon fear and eventually will lead to disillusionment.'

He remembered his initial attraction to Phoebe was through her irresistible beauty . . . . he hadn't thought too much about what else she had to offer. 'But we are attracted to the beauty of another person; it is the first thing we recognise. There is an initial attraction between two people which can lead to love.'

'Always there is a great attraction to beauty. The human mind with all its wantings and desires searches comparatively, wherever it may be, for something it can measure itself against. You compare yourself to someone who is more beautiful or more clever, who has more money than you or has a different personality, you compare ideas, philosophies, ideals and thoughts.

Everything in life has become a comparison because you will never believe in yourself completely. And so you compare the beauty of one to the beauty of another and judge if you, yourself, are worthy of owning that beauty or not. You then project your desires towards the chosen one, and if you are accepted, proceed to develop a relationship, which at some point you can call love.

Now, all this may seem a natural progression towards a good and loving relationship, but the problem arises as soon as the mind decides that this relationship is the one it wants to keep. When you are attracted to something - anything - the mental consciousness of man naturally tries to possess and control whatever it is, and indeed, once this attraction has taken hold of a relationship, freedom of living will disappear and the possibility of real love with it.

In reality, you are left with a relationship full of constraints, expectations and jealousies, a relationship which is governed by, as we have already said, a love bound with conditions. Is it any wonder that to try and love each other has become an arduous task of anxious, self-destructive proportion?'

George thought perhaps he had been blinded by what he thought was love. He never really understood all this was going on . . . . but maybe it had been and he just didn't know it. He actually did think of Phoebe as being his . . . . she was his wife . . . . they were pledged to each other, through good and bad . . . . but *they* had survived.

'As long as the mind judges, compares and tests its relationships for weakness, there can be no love. As long as the mind seeks to possess physical beauty, there can be no love, and as long as the mind depends and expects, there can be no love. The truth is, George, the mind which can be free of such patterns and see beauty in everyone and everything is also free to know real love.

You see, the human mind is told how to think. It is loaded with certain ideals and facts about life and given relevant patterns to follow, and so when it comes to seeking love it is already filled with imaginings of what love should be like. It is filled with motives of self-interest and gradually creates a means of action to fulfil its requirements.

But what it seeks is not love, it is just a projection of desires of what it believes love should be. And so we may see that love has become a series of physical and emotional sensations, a process of seeking some form of security which will bring a feeling of wellbeing into a somewhat fearful existence.'

George was astounded by all this, he needed to think about it very carefully. He was comfortable with his relationship with Phoebe and wouldn't really want to change it . . . . but he could see that with a greater understanding of love maybe their relationship could be even better.

'In a world which appears to create vast differences in people and cultures, love has become a concept which may one day break down these divisions of thinking and unite the feelings of separateness with a common bonding of oneness, but it cannot come through a self-centred, jealous, envious, possessive or dominant love. All these are processed through the mind, consequences of thought . . . . and love cannot be the outcome of thinking.

It is because the things of the mind have filled your hearts that real love is so difficult to find, and the man who lives within the accumulated knowledge and wealth of the mind may never know what love is. If the world is to find a true saviour, it will not be through intellectual thinking, it is only when the mind is quiet and thoughts have ceased, can real love be found.' . . . .

. . . . The afternoon was dragging its heels, it had only been an hour since Sonia Richmond had returned from lunch, but to her it seemed like an eternity, and to make matters worse, her computer had crashed three times already, presenting her with the tedious task of retyping the data she had lost. She glared at the monitor and muttered quietly under her breath, today things were not going well and she didn't know why.

Her thoughts, once again, were filled with Gary as she removed the next sheet from the never-shrinking 'in tray' and began entering a list of repetitive words and digits which she didn't understand, and quite frankly, didn't want to. She wondered if he would be in a business meeting. He was very intelligent, she liked that in a man . . . . but he wasn't arrogant in any way, he would take time to explain things to her with kindness and patience. She was his equal, and that made her feel good.

She recalled the day they had met for the first time. She had been sharing a quick bite of gossip in reception as she was passing through to the accounts office. Gary had appeared like a vision through the revolving doors, looking so smart and business-like in his dark suit, but with a boyish glint of enthusiasm in his eye . . . . an enthusiasm he directed towards her with devastating effect. She had fallen for him immediately, unable to resist his charming approach. It was love at first sight . . . . no doubt about it, there was something about Gary she wanted, and was going to have it, no matter the cost. Even from those first moments she had known it was the end for her and Pete, she knew they had nothing to offer each other any more.

Blinking her eyes, she turned away from the glare of her monitor and gazed across the dim room towards the old sash window, watching the drizzle bouncing off the pane of glass. Why was she feeling so anxious? Everything was fine. She was in love . . . . there was nothing to worry about. She paused for a moment, following the heavy cloud billowing in the distance before turning back to her monitor to check the input had been accepted.

She laid out her next assignment and started to read, but her concentration was being constantly interrupted with thoughts of Neville. Poor Neville, she had really been harsh with him. Her guilt began to rise again and pricked at her conscience, and with a deep sigh thought maybe she would send him a text after all, just to say sorry. She knew it would make him feel a little easier and certainly she would feel better.

Reaching across the desk she picked up her phone, activating it with positive intention. *'Hi Nev, just wanted 2 say sorry. U know I luv u really.'* She quickly entered her message, sending it on its way with a nod of approval.

Her thoughts were lighter now as she placed her phone back onto the desk and returned to her work. Looking over the long list of figures to be completed before home time, she started to type, a satisfied smile spreading across her face . . . .

. . . . With a glazed expression in his eyes, Neville Eastwood carefully lifted his glass to his lips and slurped on his fourth pint of beer, he knew deep inside he should have gone home after his third one, but something had stopped him, something had told him it didn't matter. He felt happy here, content and secure in his own little world, lounging around in a blurred, alcoholic haze of forgetfulness.

Neville had been here before. Many times he had raised a glass of beer to lighten his heavy load, and many times he had realised it was a temporary state of mind, which eventually would turn on him again. But that didn't concern him now, he would enjoy his moment of escape . . . . and suffer the consequences later.

He reached over for a new beer mat, having absentmindedly shredded the one he had been using and returned his drink to the table. He sat back surveying the room, the pub was quite empty now, only one or two tables still occupied with groups of people burdened with numerous carrier bags enjoying a coffee after a hard morning's shopping. He checked his watch, it was still early in the afternoon, perhaps too early to be drinking . . . . but he would go home after this one and sleep it off. What did it matter anyway? He had been abandoned by his sister and didn't much feel like doing anything else.

Neville sighed, again he felt alone in the world, deserted by those around him he cared for. He had always tried to please other people. From his earliest recollection he could only ever remember having a need inside to make people like him. His heart was strong with a desire to be wanted, but soon filled with hurt if he was rejected. What was it he constantly searched for . . . . but could never seem to find?

He questioned himself through the alcohol fuelled thought patterns drifting clumsily through his mind. It was easy for Sonia to criticise, she had Gary to turn to . . . . but *he* was on his own, what could he do to change things? He felt as if he had so much to give . . . . but what he *did* have was locked up inside, screaming to be released.

Gazing down at the table, he stared hopelessly at the half empty glass of beer in front of him, knowing this was not the answer. He leaned forward in a gesture to pick it up, but was interrupted by the sudden and loud ring tone of his phone. He reached over for his jacket and fumbled around inside the pockets, finally lifting it into view. The wording on the fluorescent screen showed a text from Sonia. He almost pushed it back into his pocket as he wavered a little at the thought of more abuse, but knew he would have to open it eventually so he took a deep breath and began to read.

His breathing deepened as he read the message again, lifting him above the anxiety of his clouded thoughts. It had been a kind, thoughtful message . . . . . a reminder of the love they shared. At least now he could see she cared about him. It made him feel good, and left him with a warm contentment. Maybe he was wrong to feel unwanted. Maybe everybody hid behind a negative self-impression, causing low self-esteem which prevented them from showing their true feelings.

He scratched his head and looked down at his beer again, his thoughts moving in an alcoholic blur . . . . but maybe he had hit upon some semblance of truth. If everybody could only open up a little, and truly believe in themselves . . . . then they could share that strength with others.

Picking up his glass, he gulped down the remains of his beer. He would go home now . . . . and sleep . . . .

. . . . Sonia Richmond gazed at the beautiful bunch of flowers perched precariously in the milk jug on the corner of her desk. A dozen red roses. The young delivery man had embarrassed her in front of the other girls when he had called out her name in rather a loud voice and presented them to her with a knowing wink, but now she was beaming with pride. She had squirmed, with all eyes on her, as she opened the attached card and read to herself Gary's loving message and her heart moved faster to the swaying beat of love as she had giggled to her colleagues and walked slowly back to her desk. She gazed at them, her head swirling in a torrent of happiness . . . .

. . . . 'Love is real, George. Love is the emotion your soul seeks to experience in the greatest glory. When you are confronted by your biggest fears, when you are lost in your darkest thoughts, it is love that will release you from the chains of oppression. Love without condition, love without judgement, love without need or expectation is the answer to your self-imposed imprisonment of the mind.

Love is the peace that rests behind your wasted defences. Love is the truth that dispels your cruel self-deceptions. Love is the forgiveness behind accusations and blame laid upon the shoulders of others. It is the light of your conscience, the gift of your heart, it is the breath of life which tells you everything is good. Love is the wisdom of ages, the opening door of happiness, the foundation of a world to come. It is the reason you are here, George, the purpose of your great journey through time. It is love you have come to find, in all its beauty and splendour. It is love you seek. This is what I have to tell you.'

'Wow . . . . that feels so special to hear.'

'It is special, George, it is the crowning glory upon all we have spoken about. All through our conversation we have been reaching out towards this moment . . . . when we may speak of love. It is who you are at your deepest level, and after all your trials and tribulations of life, will eventually shine out from you.'

'But love can hurt . . . . everybody feels the pain of love.'

'Love cannot hurt you, it is *the* emotion which is free of pain. The hurt you feel is from the *conditions* you have placed upon it. Love should be free to extend itself without expectation and, if it is allowed to grow unconditionally, will give you, in return, this same freedom. It is a blossoming flower which awaits your attention, and will bring to you a peace from life that will raise you high above your anxious thoughts.

Can you imagine what your relationships would be like if you were to remove from them the obstacles which make them uncertain? If you were to cease with your jealous accusations and forget the unfulfilled desires you have laid so neatly at the feet of others? Can you not see the burden you have placed upon each other; the blame and judgement hanging like a noose around your necks as you seek to fulfil the requirements of love?

Have you never considered how your children would grow if you were to show them a love of understanding, allowing them to evolve with high self-esteem and without fear of loss? To teach them love is unconditional would be to give them the greatest gift in life, for it is their earliest concern that once they have given their love, it will not be returned.

Over many thousands of years of evolution man has cried out for an answer to his pain. He has taken for himself every possible comfort, sacrificed gladly to his chosen deity, fought his wars in the name of peace and destroyed all he had no care for . . . . but still he searches for an answer. Is it so difficult to believe that love can change everything?'

'I suppose we do try to love . . . . but as you say, maybe we don't understand it.' George mused with some concern.

'You see, life is a great tidal wave of energy flowing from the outer to the inner, and back from the inner to the outer. This is a constant flow of life energy which gives movement to your world by creating action in the outer and reaction in the inner.

Imagine you have filled your mind with knowledge, an accumulation of conditioned ideals and cultural, traditional morals which have made you blind to anything in your outer world which is different from your own formulation of life. You are aware of living, but only through a narrow blinkered vision, which reflects in both inner and outer. And so a conflict has arisen between what you believe is real and what you actually see, a conflict which builds up inside a consequence of emotional pain and anxiety.

This is the world you have made for yourselves, a world of contrasting ideas and ideals and until you are able to let go of the 'self' which believes it holds all the answers, conflict must always occur between your inner and outer worlds. It is the innocent mind that can release conflict, it is the innocent mind that can know love.'

George was considering closely his own mind and the many times he had argued in the past to try and make himself look better than others, but he could see now, it was a pointless thing to do and quite often brought upset to everyone, himself included.

'Many people live their lives by following the actions of others, they are drawn into a thought system which is not of their own making, but follow blindly, even though they may see it is not suitable for them. They are coerced into belief systems which are inappropriate and damaging to the mind. Thoughts attract like thoughts and so it is important to be master of your mind to be in control of your own destiny.

If your thoughts are heavy, change them through your actions. The creative process of life; thought, word and deed, is quite interchangeable and can easily be reversed, allowing actions to influence your verbal interaction, and consequently your thinking.

You may be quite surprised how loving, caring intentions are easily transmitted between each other, giving rise to loving relationships'

George knew he wasn't a big romantic or the sort of person who would be affectionate all the time, but he had noticed this was true; the more effort you made to give love, the more it seemed to come back to you. The trouble was that he was usually under so much stress that he had difficulty demonstrating love in the first place.

'Cultivate an awareness of observing your outer world without judgement or condemnation. Allow the world to be free and express itself without interference from your own point of self-justification, without criticism by conditioned, superficial prejudice. When you can freely observe with an open mind, with true innocence of intent, there is a freedom which rises within your inner world, a freedom of understanding, beauty and love. Give love to the world you see . . . . and love will be returned, ten fold.'

Suddenly he had an urge to speak, an urge to let the voice know how he was feeling. 'This is wonderful, talking to you like this . . . . about life . . . . about the things that matter in life . . . . you are giving me so much to take away with me, so much that will certainly help me to change . . . . it is just . . . . well, it is just wonderful.' He felt better now, opening up and releasing his true feelings, for too long he had been hiding inside the good part of his nature.

'You are already changing, George, you are already changing because you have realised many things about the human race, and consequently many things about yourself. Sometimes change is purely a recognition of what you have become, with a clear understanding that this is *not* who you are.

As I say, it is enough to observe your thoughts, observe your actions without commitment to right or wrong, good or bad. Pay attention to the outer world with all its falsities and pettiness, all its fears and jealousies, it will show you the activities of your own mind and body, making you aware of your own thoughts and feelings. From this outer awareness you will come to the inner, from observing who you are not, you will discover who you are, and out of such awareness there comes a clarity which is not made possible by thought or by intellectual reasoning.

Out of this awareness it is possible to know a love without condition and therefore a love without separation or time or fear. When you can know this love, George, you will know freedom from the 'self' and an immeasurable peace and communion with the outer world.' . . . .

. . . . Again, Adam Katowycz grasped at his teeshirt, roughly pulling it upwards towards his swollen face, wiping away his tears. He couldn't remember the last time he had cried. It must have been when he was a child, when his father had left, knowing he may never see him again. Even so, he remembered the salty wetness of his cheeks as tears rolled from his eyes, and the unmistakable feeling of hopelessness rising up through his chest clutching at his erratic breathing.

He stared blankly at the over-flowing ashtray where the burned out remnants of tobacco were still laid in the shape of the cigarette he had abandoned, his crumpled jacket, dropped untidily onto the floor beside his bed, and at his shoes angrily kicked across the room. He watched the blinking, light-filled stars on his monitor as they pulsated and exploded, filtering away into oblivion.

He felt nothing. His whole being consumed with a total feeling of emptiness devouring him like some alien predator. He gulped and tried to breathe deeper, but the tears had risen again, leaving him helpless. Rolling over in defiance, he held his breath, trying desperately to repress his tears. He had to stop. He must think clearly.

Pushing his head deep into his pillow, he tried to smother his fearful emotions . . . . but he couldn't stop the anguish of his tears from falling . . . .

. . . . Catherine Katowycz suddenly picked up the television remote control resting on her lap and turned off the volume, she couldn't concentrate knowing there was something wrong with Adam, she had seen it in his face and could feel a heavy atmosphere in the air. Usually, when she felt uneasy, she would dismiss it, thinking it was her imagination. But this time was different. She had seen the troubled look of pain in Adam's eyes, and felt it sweep over her as he ran up the stairs. This time she knew it was real . . . . but she didn't know what to do.

Tiptoeing quietly to the foot of the stairs, she listened carefully, but could hear nothing. Maybe she would risk the blast of his temper and go up to see if he was okay . . . . she had a right to know . . . . she was his mother.

Catherine climbed tentatively up the staircase, her heart pounding, listening carefully as she approached Adam's room. She could hear no movement and stepped closer to the door. Maybe he *was* alright. Maybe she had been wrong again. Placing her ear to the door, she suddenly heard a strange muffled cry and instinctively straightened her back and gently knocked. 'Adam . . . . are you alright? I'm coming in.' She turned the handle and stepped forward, slowly opening the door. 'Oh, Adam, what's wrong son? . . . . Can't you tell me what's wrong? . . . . I only want to help.' Her voice cracked as she stuttered on her words, distress rising in her heart. 'Oh, son . . . . please tell me what's wrong . . . . please let me help.'

Catherine fell down next to her boy's weeping torso and put her arms around his shoulders. 'Please, Adam . . . . let me love you.' . . . .

. . . . Pulling the pillow tightly into his face, Adam Katowycz clutched despairingly for comfort in the soft fabric. He inhaled deeply to steady the irregular thump of his heart, releasing his breath slowly into the heaviness of the room. Rubbing his eyes, he turned over, clenching his fists in a desperate attempt to hide the fever of pain surging through his body. It was too late to hide. It was too late for regrets.

Adam's wide, hollow eyes stared hopelessly at the door, pleading for an understanding of his plight as he heard the knock and watched helplessly as his mother stepped in and slowly walked over to him. Panic raced up and down his body, raising his defences with fears of reprimand . . . . and then, a silent moment of calm, a moment when his heart slowed and his thoughts were of assurance. He felt his mother's arms surround him with a warmth of feeling, easing his pain with a tender caress. For a moment, he was exactly where he wanted to be; carefully protected inside the womb of his mother's love.

He reached out and buried his head deep into the bosom of her caring arms, tears bursting from his eyes in a torrent of relief. He gazed at her, but didn't hear her words. He was lost . . . . deeply lost within a moment he could never explain . . . .

. . . . 'There is a love deep inside you, George, a love which will not be denied. A love which reaches out from the depth of your soul with forgiveness for, and understanding of all the injustice you have placed upon it. It is the love you seek to experience as you evolve through every misconception of life, and finally will be the love you recognise as your true state of being. This is the love resting deeply within the soul and is the constant radiation of the universal presence that is its very essence. Real love is a part of the oneness where all is accepted and loved.

As you awaken, your love will begin to expand, changing your relationships for the better. You will find it is possible to love with a wise heart that will empower others, operating from the calm, compassionate and loving peace of your soul. It is the total surrender of all negative thoughts and emotions that stand in the way of love.

Real love is the bond you will create by listening to the voice inside you, for this is where the truth of love can be found . . . . through your alignment with the higher forces of your nature.

All your relationships serve to help you remove the obstacles you have placed in the way of real, soul love. The needs and expectations laid before your relationships are the conditions of love requested by your personality and not from the true soul you are. It is when you can stop trying to change the people you are with, and recognise them from a much deeper level, that you will find the true essence of love will prevail.

Real love is a feeling from the soul, a presence which allows a relationship to blossom in its own perfect way, with an understanding it is the evolution of love which is important, and not the likes and dislikes of the personality.

There are no external forms of love that can bring you lasting joy . . . . the personality is never happy for long, when its desires are fulfilled, it will certainly come up with a list of new ones. However, when you are open to receive the true essence of love, it can come to you from anyone and everyone, bringing you true joy and lasting happiness.

Allow yourself the understanding that everyone loves you at the deepest level of the soul, although, of course, this may sometimes be difficult to believe at the human level. But, if you have a strong 'knowing' of the truth, it is much easier to look beyond petty hostilities and receive energies from a higher place.

It is time for you all to reclaim the true power which lies beneath the surface of 'your story'. Let go of the 'victim' you have claimed to be yourself - it is not who you are. Release the blame you have attached to others when life has not gone the way you expected, for I will tell you once again, George, everything in your life, without exception, is a true reflection of what is inside your head and inside your heart. There is nothing outside of you that has not been created from the inside. Feel good about yourself and reclaim the wonderful creative power which has been lost for far too long behind the false image you hold of yourself and everyone else. The reality you choose is the reality you will have.'

George interrupted, wanting to get something off his chest. 'Everything you say seems to resonate as true with something inside me, but . . . . maybe I still have a fear of not being good enough to change.'

'For most people the word 'change' raises fear within. It is a belief that to change means to lose something. Something held dear, believing it to be a sacrifice. Of course, this is not true, but sometimes it is only after the change has been made, and the fears have been dispelled, can clarity be seen, and if the giving up of something creates a feeling of sacrifice, then perhaps you are not quite ready to let go of it.

Evolution *is* change, and will come about whether you are open to it or not, but speed of change on an individual basis may be controlled without pain, without sacrifice and in a manner which is pleasing and comfortable. Try to relax about life and let your focus be on what you desire instead of what you do not.

To create what you desire in life, in any relationship, you need to hold a vision of what you would like to see. Most people visualise what they *do not* want to see, and then complain. It is your own thoughts and actions which draw certain behaviours from other people. Remember this and make it your practice to display a true feeling of who you are. View other peoples' actions as you would a mirror and learn to discover what their behaviour is telling you about yourself.

To change life is to change the way you are interacting with all around you. It is not a sacrifice to project an image to the world which is of the highest nature you can be.'

Again, George could see how he had cut himself off from other people, so filled with his own disappointments and fears of life. He had built a wall around himself which had become difficult to break down, difficult for anybody to reach him. His thoughts raced away to his relationship with Phoebe, his children . . . . he was making it so hard for them to see the true George . . . . so hard for them to love him.

'You have forgotten the simplicity of life, George, you have become accustomed to bracing yourself and reacting the best you can when life turns on you. The simplicity is: Life is the mirror through which you can observe the dramas inside, life is a reflection of something *you* are doing to *yourself.*

If you will recognise the moment-to-moment choices you are making in life, then change would be a natural occurrence for the better. But love will release you, love will effect change in the whole of life.

Can you believe deep inside, there awaits the greatest force of energy known to humankind, with such grace and beauty it will manifest a different way of thinking for the entire world. Hidden behind your mask of sorrow is a joy of astonishing grandeur waiting patiently to be released. This is your journey, George, to meet and blend with the essence of your soul, the essence of love. And, of course, as with all journeys, you must prepare yourself for what is ahead.

Make a start by releasing the forms of energy which do not fit who you wish to become. Observe yourself closely. Look for the old patterns and habits you want to let go and replace them with a new vision. Listen to your heart and hear the voice of conscience guiding you forward with every breath. Listen to love . . . . it will not let you down . . . .

. . . .Settling herself on the sofa, Phoebe Eastwood eagerly removed the lid of the silver and white box and carefully lifted the tissue paper covering the white leather album. She started to glow with excitement, a big smile rising across her face as she balanced it on her lap and slowly began to turn the pages.

She couldn't believe how she had looked thirty years ago, so young and innocent, and grinning up at her from the next page was George, arriving at the church, so handsome with the wind ruffling his thick black hair. He was with his best man, Larry Webster, someone she hadn't liked too much, a bad influence on George she had decided, but his speech had been funny and quite emotional, as though he really cared.

She remembered the wonderful feeling of anticipation as she had stood with her father and two bridesmaids at the top of the aisle, waiting for the wedding music to play and the feeling of relief when the weather had stayed fine for the outside group photographs. She chuckled to herself, glancing at the hairstyles and fashion of the times.

It all came flooding back to her, such a grand affair, she recalled. She lifted her cup of tea, her little finger poised delicately out to the side. Over the page were cousins, aunties and uncles and even friends they hadn't seen for years . . . . they had all been there for their big day . . . . weddings were wonderful occasions for bringing people together.

Phoebe scanned each photograph. It was strange, looking at people who were not around any more; her parents, uncle Bill, auntie Sadie, all now passed away. It was difficult to believe they had ever existed, but she could feel them rising in her memory as she pondered their photographs and felt their energy again. She sipped gently from her raised cup and placed it down again on the coffee table.

Fumbling around in the bottom of the box, she found a loose assortment of snapshots taken at the reception and drunken, red-eyed polaroid pictures from the end of the evening's dancing. The strange poses and ridiculous facial expressions of the wine-weary guests made her smile and shake her head in disbelief. She sighed deeply at the regimented portraits as the bride and groom beamed into the camera. These were wonderful photographs, she must show George, he would love to see them again. She sipped delicately on her tea as her mind filled with happy memories from the past. They had had little money then . . . . they had little money now . . . . but at least their love had survived the test of time.

Phoebe turned back to the official photographs in the album and stared endlessly at the portrait of the bride in her ivory satin dress. Behind her glasses tears welled in her blue eyes as her mind was pulled back into the emotion of the day. She was such a young girl, barely twenty, her blond hair so naturally wavy. She peered closely at her face, not a wrinkle in sight, maybe just a touch of dark shadow underneath her eyes, from quite a sleepless night, she recalled.

She tucked the album under her arm and stood up from the sofa, walking over to the wrought iron circular mirror hanging above the sideboard and looked at her face. She sighed again and inhaled deeply, dismissing the few wrinkles she had as a fact of life. She laughed to herself and spun round, jumping back on the sofa, feeling quite sprightly for her fifty years and her thoughts inevitably moved back to George. How could anybody live with *him* for thirty years and not have a few wrinkles to show for it?

She bit her bottom lip and playfully flipped open the album. The young face of George gazed back at her as she relaxed back into the soft cushion and closed her eyes. But they still loved each other, that was the important thing, they loved each other without either of them having to say it. It had been written in tablets of stone somewhere, she knew that, and so must George. Even though he was sometimes difficult, she loved him . . . . he was a part of her at a very deep level, beyond the day to day bickering and self-centred wantings.

Their wedding day had been wonderful, the perfect time to show their friends and families how they loved each other . . . . to a point where sometimes it could hurt. Phoebe remembered the pain she had put herself through when she had thought she may lose his love. It was different now, much easier and more comforting to know the love they shared was real and couldn't be destroyed.

She glanced again at the bride and groom and allowed herself a little smile. Love without fear is the way love *should* be . . . . she knew this with certainty in her heart.

BE HAPPY

'Many years ago, a man who had everything
visited a market in North Africa.
As he approached the market and walked
between the camels and dancers,
fire eaters and mystics, a young beggar appeared before him.

"Oh great master; you who have everything,
I have not eaten for two days, please could you help me?"
said the beggar.
And the man with everything replied angrily,
"I did not accumulate vast wealth and
prosperity by giving away the things
that are dear to me, go away and beg elsewhere!"

"But please master; you who have everything,
please spare a coin for me so I may live another day.
For in return I will give you eternal happiness."

And the man said,
"How may I trust you, beggar boy, when you have nothing to give?"
Upon this, the boy took a wooden box from his sack
and handed it to the man.
"See, here is the box containing eternal happiness,
hold it in your arms and you will know."

With this, the man picked up the box
and a great feeling of happiness came over him.
The greatest feeling of happiness he had ever known,
and his heart was filled with joy and love,
and his lust for the box so fierce, he gave the beggar a coin and left.

The man walked with the box into the market town,
and there he ate, drank and made merry and shared his happiness
with all who would share with him.

And, as night fell, he returned to his hotel
and upon reaching his room, he sat upon his bed and opened the box.

The box contained nothing.'

'You see, the truth is, George, when you have looked hard and long upon the world, and taken all you can from it to try and satisfy your needs, when you have smothered yourselves in materialistic gain and wandered helplessly through the trials and tribulations of ritualistic relationships, when you have lifted yourselves high with promise of better days and fallen heavily from self-imposed abuse and disorders, and, when you have considered the million and one other things it appears you have to do . . . . then you will grind to a halt in exhaustion . . . . with happiness still tantalisingly out of reach.'

George sat up straight and closed the book he had taken from one of the many wooden shelves surrounding him, watching the pulsating light with its many colours flowing along his arms. 'Carry on. I'm listening.' He spoke softly into the vast ceilings of the great Library with a desire to hear as much as possible.

'When you have contemplated life time and time again and concluded that each and every thing you attach yourself to in the world is only a temporary release from your fears, then you will find the happiness you seek is beyond all you see. You will find the answer to your quest was here all the time, waiting silently within. Like the beautiful fragrance of a flower, true happiness is an expression of your true self.'

Michael and Lynda Goodwin   164

'But why *can't* we be happy, if happiness is inside us . . . . surely it must be easy to do?'

'Most people believe, as I have said, that happiness is an external experience gained by fulfilment of personal needs and materialistic wealth. Sometimes, it is only when all is lost, that true happiness may be seen to be alive and well. Sometimes, it is only when every other avenue has been exhausted, can true happiness be found. But always, it will be discovered by a shift in thought which allows love to guide your life . . . . happiness is the natural consequence of *real* love.

Many people are afraid of happiness, believing it to be a fleeting glimpse of a state that will not last, and spend their time pessimistically waiting for its demise. They may say, 'This is too good to be true', and prepare themselves for the fall which takes them back into their fears and disillusioned ways, leaving a continuing doubt that happiness can exist at all.

Others reflect upon happy experiences from the past which are now gone, and believe they will return at a future time, when certain conditions and requirements of life have been met. They trust that happiness may be collected by achievements and dream that one day they may have a storeroom full of it, which will open up on demand. But it is a false dream which leads them on and on with its promise of utopian value . . . . for they doubt happiness as much as they doubt themselves.

It is, indeed, a great irony of truth to say: That which you most desire, brings about the worst of your fears. But, it is a truth you have learned to live with.'

'It seems madness to me that we are afraid of happiness . . . . but, you are right in what you say.' George could recognise only too well the truth in the voice's word. He couldn't remember the last time he had felt any glimpse of true happiness, it did always seem to be a constant battle looking for something he believed would bring it into his life, and certainly there had been nothing recently to do that.

'Yes, but not only have you learned to be afraid of happiness, you have also learned to feel very guilty about it. Too much happiness is far from recognised as the pure, natural state it is, and is regarded as being wrong when there is so much suffering in the world. You have been taught from a very early age that it is alright to be happy occasionally . . . . but anything over and beyond this may evoke a high repayment of misery. Hence, you keep your fingers crossed and avoid walking under ladders to keep the cruel hand of fate at bay.

The fear of happiness has sadly been passed down through the generations, each one elaborating on myths and superstitions, until it has become a myth itself to believe continued happiness is possible. Everyone is very certain they would like to be happy, but there remains a great confusion as to how this can be done.

However, your confusion is conditioned, and is in no way inherent within your true self. It is simply a part of your story, a part of the false self you will leave behind as your evolution progresses.

To do this, it is firstly important for you to understand the misperception of what happiness really is, and to know in your heart there are no prerequisites for you to be happy. There is nothing of real value that can stand between you and your happiness . . . . only your own belief there is.'

'So you can tell me how to find happiness?'

'Quite the contrary. What I am telling you is that the pursuit of happiness is a grave mistake. To continually seek something real which you cannot find, is, in effect, a denial that it exists at all. It is an illusion of the mind; a trick of the false self which makes you believe everything good is outside yourself. The world *does not* hold your happiness - it is inside you, and, therefore, to try and chase that which you already have . . . . must end in failure. It is important for you to completely understand this, George.'

'Yes, I am understanding perfectly. Don't forget I am the one who has spent his entire life chasing happiness! I can see now how pointless it has been.' George nodded in total agreement.

'That is good. If you can remember happiness is the effect caused by the love you feel inside, then you have a starting point to observe your mental and emotional state of being.'

'You mean if I am not feeling happy, I am not feeling love?'

'At the deepest level, yes, this is the truth of the matter, but many people would argue differently and blame circumstances of life for lack of happiness. This philosophy would suggest that the attainment of happiness is ultimately 'out of your own hands', and that your happiness is 'good' only so long as you judge the circumstances of your life to be good. On the other hand, the circumstances of life looked upon as 'bad' would quickly change your emotional state to one of sadness. Here are the two extremes of polarities - but it is *your* decision as to which one you will experience. The world cannot take away your right to happiness or sadness, it is a choice *you* will make . . . . a choice you will make through *fear* or *love*.'

'Yes, I can see this now, we have already spoken of it. The strange thing for me is the understanding that *I* am in control of my feelings, and not a victim of fate. I had always believed that life just happened . . . . and that I should act accordingly. Somehow, it gives me confidence to look at my life more closely and change it for the better.'

'There is a great freedom, George, which comes with this knowledge, a freedom which allows you to be whoever you may choose. The world may often appear to be trying very hard to take this choice away . . . . but truly, it cannot. This new freedom of thought is the doorway to the experience of a new self; a confident self of wise understanding and compassion; a self of high esteem and self-worth.'

George thought carefully for a moment. 'If I were to be honest with you, honest with myself, I mean, I would say self-worth has been something that has troubled me all my life. You see, I have always felt unworthy or not good enough in many ways . . . . but now I am starting to understand why.'

'Feelings of unworthiness are suffered by many, many people. They are, again, a result of the conditioned criticisms and judgements placed upon you as children, time and time again, until you believed them to be true. In fact, not only have you listened to someone else and believed what you heard, you have learned to judge, criticise and condemn yourself, and no matter how hard anyone else has ever judged you, it is you who have judged yourself the hardest.

This constant self-judgement is also something you have learned, and is not natural to you, but the effect of its cruel ways is making you unhappy. Judgement has become a way of life, preventing you from seeing *anything* as it really is. It has clouded your ability to see the beauty and strength of your true self, and left you looking at a self that 'could do better' and 'could be more'. In effect, what you *do* see is a reflection of your judgements. This is not the truth, but you have learned to believe it as so.'

Looking back at his childhood again, he could recall the feeling of pressure put on him by his father. He had been criticised and made to feel he could never do anything that would come up to his father's expectations. It had been a disciplined upbringing and George believed it had encouraged him to do better . . . . he had even done the same thing with Neville . . . . but perhaps unknowingly had broken his own son's confidence. A great feeling of remorse struck the pit of his stomach and he swallowed hard with a promise to do better.

'The false self believes that judgement can give you something extra; some edge of cleverness that others cannot find. It is convinced that without judgement it will fall behind and become disadvantaged, and so seeks to be one step ahead at any time with its cynical criticisms. After a while, the judgemental self finds it is engaged in extremes of competitiveness, with attitudes of social comparison, envy and jealousy, leaving it with a desperate never-ending search for happiness.

The cycle of constant self-judgement can become very destructive and may only be broken by learning to love yourself again. Like all forms of illness and unhappiness, it is simply a call for love, and at some point, you will choose between your cruel conditioning and the love of your true self.'

'I hear clearly what you are saying, but surely there are times when we have to judge ourselves as wrong?'

'It is one thing to judge your behaviour as 'not good enough', but quite another to judge your self as 'not good enough'. All things are perceived and dealt with according to your level of understanding. If you have behaved in such a way that is not who you want to be, then you have made a 'bad' decision, it does not mean you have become a 'bad' person. You may judge that you have made mistakes in your past, but they are not your identity - *you* are not your mistakes. In truth, you are the one who is observer of all you declare 'good' and 'bad'; the one who is willing to release your mistakes with love.

This is the process for undoing your self-judgements and self-doubt, by replacing your thoughts of fear with thoughts of love, thoughts of condemnation with thoughts of kindness, thoughts of doubt with thoughts of trust. *You* are the transformation that will heal the disjointed, conditioned self and lift it out of the shadows and into the true light of wholeness. It is a process by which you will forgive yourself and then extend your forgiveness out into the world.'

Listening to the voice, George was starting to feel a little better about himself, knowing that his actions were 'inbred' into his subconscious, and that it wasn't *him* being a bad person. He never wanted to be seen as anything but good, nobody did, he was sure of this now, but, of course, he could make mistakes the same as everyone else. 'But would you say we need to accept ourselves a little more?' He could already see the way forward.

'Well done, George, you are leading me nicely into the conversation, and yes, it is important for everybody to accept who they are at any moment in time. But this does not include accepting yourself as a bad person just because you have made a few mistakes. It is essential you remember who you really are and accept you are a 'work in progress' evolving towards the beauty of the true self. In fact, it is your level of self-acceptance which will determine the level of your happiness. In other words, you will enjoy as much happiness as you believe you are worthy of. Again, when self-acceptance is low, it is easy to fall into a circle of thought which pushes away the belief that you deserve to be happy, and, consequently, out of this low attitude, you will suffer as much pain as you also believe you are worthy of.

The important thing for you to remember is that whatever you may feel uneasy with, whatever feelings you have of unrest and unworthiness, it is true to say they are unreal, and belong to the self that has been conditioned many times to believe many unrealities of itself.'

'Is this the reason why we feel so guilty, because we feel unworthy of having better things?'

'Guilt is a way of life to many people and is built upon total beliefs of unworthiness. The false self feels guilty about happiness because it feels guilty about everything. Pleasure is a happiness of the body; an enjoyment of the senses, but along the way you have learned to believe that pleasure is of the devil. You have built up false morals about everything you consider pleasurable. Money is 'the root of all evil' you will tell yourselves, and laughter 'will end in tears', success will be 'the ruin of you' and that 'the devil makes use of idle hands'. All this and more you have been told . . . . and all this you have believed.

It is a self-imposed suffering of the cruellest endeavour, a suffering which you have allowed to remove every glimpse of happiness you have ever stumbled across. But, your suffering is not real, it is a fabrication of fear given to you from birth by others who have fallen into the same suffering. You have repeated the same patterns, the same ideas, developed the same habits over and over again, until your story has become a mixed up, pitiful tale.

George interjected. 'Again, we are coming to the same conclusions as before, all our problems stem from the fact that we are stuck inside behavioural patterns which have been bred into us from birth, everything we do is somehow lost and inadequate because of it. I can see this very clearly now, it is madness.' He surprised himself a little with his appraisal of the situation.

'It is madness indeed, but unless you can see the madness with a clear vision, it will continue. From the very outset you are made to feel weak, inadequate and isolated human beings, and so you seek to be happy through something external. You believe happiness is hiding in companionship, in ideas, in achievements, in special relationships, but even though you have tried your best to unravel the mystery, life has taken you full circle, back into your loneliness, with any signs of happiness you may have stumbled upon long since disappeared. And so you tell yourself you are not 'good' enough, you blame a weakness of personality for the painful dilemma you have caused and then dust yourself off to start your search all over again.

You are quite correct with your comments, George, it is true, we again arrive at the same conclusion, the same point of observation that tells you very clearly there is something about the 'old habits', the 'repetitive patterns' of living which are faulty, and clearly no longer serve any purpose other than to keep you fixed into a cycle of chaotic action.

Your search for happiness is no different to your desire for peace or your longing to be loved, it is thwarted by a mind which digs deep into a memory of past events and relives the same experiences time and time again, like a dull machine which has no choice in anything it does.

Inwardly you are dependent on so many things for your happiness, and, when life is going your way, you do not want to change, but when the dependence starts to hurt you, when the things you have depended upon have left you or bring you pain, then you want to be free.

There is only one way to recognise happiness, and that is to *be* happy by releasing the false self you have become and renew the old way of thinking which has beaten your mind into the confusion you can see all around. Observe your true self with the attention it seeks and allow thoughts of old memories and traditions to be erased.

If your heart is open to change, George, then you will hear my words . . . . and when you have thought about them carefully perhaps you will decide to start again with your earth life, but with a different vision to the one you had before. Perhaps now you would look upon life in a much kinder way, with a better understanding of how good life can be . . . . I believe the time has come now for you to make your decision . . . .

WHATEVER HAPPENED TO GEORGE?

'. . . . . . and at the end of it all
it is only each other we see . . . . . .
and the reflection is of love.'

With the broadest of smiles flashing across his face, George glanced down at the unfashionable camel overcoat resting neatly on the shiny polished surface of the rosewood table. His thoughts had been somewhere else, drifting in and out of the subject matter he and the voice had been discussing, but his overcoat with its almost shabby appearance and bottom button missing had pulled his senses back towards the world he had come from.

His eyes narrowed a little as he called to mind the accident which had brought him here in the first place, but that seemed such a long time ago . . . . or was it? He couldn't be sure about anything any more. Instinctively he pulled back his jacket sleeve, but then remembered his watch had stopped, coincidentally at the time of the accident, but shook his head slowly with the realization that there were no coincidences here . . . . in this special place.

He picked up his hat and proceeded to prod and squeeze it with finger and thumb, trying to reshape the top of it, but after numerous attempts to bend the rim and push out the pointed bit at the front, it still looked exactly as before with no change at all. He tossed it with careful precision to rest precariously between his overcoat collar and the edge of the table and almost applauded himself for his accuracy of aim, but immediately dismissed it as childish behaviour and focused his attention back onto the matter in hand.

He was happy, elated in fact, knowing that soon he would be returning to his earth life. He knew he would soon be back with Phoebe and his kids, and that was such a feeling that he couldn't help but allow himself a little excitement to burn through his veins, after all, the voice had said as much, and he remembered the slight flutter of his heart and quickening of his breathing as the conversation had ended.

What would Phoebe make of all this? How would he begin to explain about the accident . . . . this beautiful Library . . . . the voice? He coughed and slowly gazed upward into the heavens of the room, trying hard to record the majesty of his vision into his memory for future reference. He breathed deeply on the sweet fragrance of jasmine and gardenia, the intimate perfumes which had meant so much to him all those years ago. How could he begin to relate such an experience of peace and mystic beauty into a world of total chaos?

He smiled knowingly, as if he had been privy to a huge secret, and stretched out his long legs, tapping gently with his toe against the brass hinges of his leather briefcase. What about the job interview? He had pushed it away deep into the recesses of his mind as if it were something from the past, which then concerned him . . . . but now didn't seem to matter at all. He had moved on, way beyond the chatter of anxious thoughts and hopeful expectation of the life he had left behind . . . . but it was easy to say that in this peaceful place, it was easy to feel calm in the harmonious energies surrounding him with such a loving feeling of warmth and comfort.

George knew the job interview didn't matter enough for him to be anxious in any way, it was just a part of the life he had made for himself on earth, a part of his life which would lead him to some sort of experience, but now he knew he wouldn't name that experience as being 'good' or 'bad'. He had learned to accept whatever came his way in a much more passive manner, by realising that to fight against the world was actually to fight against himself . . . . and he had spent far too many years of his life doing just that.

He pulled back his legs, withdrawing his attention from the briefcase, the narrow cut of material pulling slightly at the knee as he placed one leg over the other and pushed his shoulders gently back into the soft velvet crush.

The voice had spoken of many things and he was proud of the way he had listened, and especially proud of the way he could understand such inspirational conversations and their fundamental importance to his own well-being and to the society he lived in.

Already he felt differently about life, he had changed inside without particularly trying to change anything. Just by listening closely to the conversation and observing his thoughts he had been able to open up and clearly see that many things on the earth were not right and that many beliefs he had held were just nonsense. He had learned that sometimes just to step away a little from the action of his mind and, as the voice would say, observe without judgement, it was possible to recognise the truth. He could now see very clearly that the human species was mostly stuck in habitual ways with confused mental attitudes . . . . and even with high intellectual prowess and advanced technology, still had a long way to go to find any form of lasting happiness. Here, in this extraordinary place, he had found an awareness to see all this.

Now he understood the evolution of man from the instinctive mind and physical consciousness through to the opening up of the mental consciousness. He had been able to comprehend how man progressed in one direction of intelligence, and how that intelligence inwardly started to destroy the mind with absurd fears and emotional darkness. He could see how man was being brainwashed, conditioned to live by certain nationalistic views and ideals, responding hopelessly to cultural rules and explanations of life which were totally inadequate . . . . man had become filled with fears of his own making.

He slowed down his thoughts and cast them back towards his younger years. As a child he had felt 'no fear'. It was a positive period of his life with little to bother him, and he remembered quite readily that the future was of no consequence to a young person discovering life on a day by day basis. He recalled life had been an adventure each moment, bringing with it new and different experiences to excite him as he moved towards adulthood.

But the grown George had changed, lost somewhere in a battle against his world, trying to prove his worth in a society which expected everything. His thoughts had changed, they could no longer accept living without constant analysis of life, always reaching out for something more. Long gone were the childhood days filled with little care.

He had become narrow-minded because his consciousness had been conditioned within boundaries of 'right' and 'wrong', 'do this' and 'don't do that'. It had all been put together by thought building up a false self with a false identity and conflicting images about life. He had understood this much of the conversation well, and once recognised, it was clear to see that it was everywhere, in every walk of life.

The 'Story of George'. He liked this explanation and could totally see the implications of it. Systematically he had arrived at an image about himself and then had built a story around that image to compete in a world that, by comparison, appeared to be against him. Man had created a centre which separated him from the rest and then looked upon the world through a divided logic of 'me' and 'you', 'us' and 'them'. It was simple really, while ever man lived his life through a 'self' centre, it was not possible to break down any barriers towards a peaceful existence. While ever man's thoughts were focused on his own story, he would always stand alone, constantly fighting a battle against himself and society.

This was something George certainly should get clear in his mind, and try to consider the whole movement of life as one thing which he shared with everyone, this would be a fundamental step towards peace, both inner and outer. He uncrossed his legs and stretched them out again, still excited and astounded by his new-found understanding.

'Know who you are', the voice had said it many times, but the real truth of the statement was only just beginning to fully sink in. How could man be free following blindly the rituals and beliefs of a society which was so obviously biased? Surely it was the mind that could look beyond the limits of psychological conditioning that could know itself?

Suddenly George felt lighter as this realisation of truth filtered through his being. For him to move forward, it was a matter of respectfully looking at the old habitual energies he had been given by society . . . . including his parents . . . . and evolving them through a new positive movement of thought. His mind lingered optimistically around the vision of a new George, a less anxious and more confident person, free to live a new life with belief and hope for the future.

His eyes sparkled as he again allowed himself time to gaze around the great room, his breathing softened by the gracious atmosphere. He wanted to find peace in the world, everybody wanted to live in peace, but how could this be when the world was in such conflict?

His thoughts fell back to the brave soldier, all those years ago fighting for something he believed would change everything, but ultimately realising that nothing good could ever be achieved through the hostilities of war. He closed his eyes momentarily in remembrance of such a waste of life, such a pitiful encounter of violence . . . . . . and then opened them passionately with an urge to fulfil the soldier's longings of a peaceful world. If it was possible to use the past as a declaration of support for a new way of life, then he would try his best to make it so.

He felt a slight swell of anger and frustration rise into his emotional state before realising he had to forgive the past . . . . . . he had to forgive the helpless state of mind which had brought about such hostilities. He now understood his own anger was a form of violence, an internal form of attack, the very same emotional feeling which created conflict between countries. Anger was a reaction against something you would not try to understand, a barrier of defence against a perceived attack.

How delicate the human mind had become to be so fearful of even a wrong word. How frail the intelligence of man could be to allow such trivia to destroy his peace. George could clearly recall the voice's words. If only man could release the tension of his fearful thoughts, if he could find the innocence that would allow him to forgive with humility and compassion, then he would be free from his constant pain. All men were born with an innocent nature, children were so pure and innocent with love for everything and everybody, it was not until they were told to think otherwise did the problem start to unfold.

He deliberated on his recollections, knowing they were right and true because they made him feel good inside, they lifted his heart with a strong belief that this was the way forward, this was the only way man could evolve into a higher consciousness. It made him feel lighter with a new energy . . . . a true purpose to continue building a better life.

He stopped for a moment to check himself. Could this really be the same George who had become so lost within his world; the same George who had stumbled along trying hopelessly to dig something good out of his life? He felt more assured now, able to start again and release the past, living each moment as it came to him. He would learn to flow with life and, after all, he had his own guardian angel, his own true voice from deep within, helping him, guiding him forward . . . . how could he deny this now . . . . after this inspirational experience?

Of course, he knew it wouldn't be the same as here in the Library, but through his feelings, through his intuition, he would know which way to turn. He would know the way of love . . . . just by how he was feeling. Life was a process, a path towards finding love . . . . real love, and George could feel now he was very ready to walk that path.

Contentment filled his inner being as his positive thoughts settled into his emotions. Yes, he could understand that love with conditions and expectations was a false love, he could see that dependence and attachment to relationships would inevitably bring about jealousies and raise fears of abandonment, but he knew it was a start, and that ultimately caring for each other could only lead to better relationships with real love the true objective.

How he missed Phoebe . . . . he would never have thought he could want to be with her so much, but he knew he had to take this feeling back with him and not just take her for granted. He felt a deep sense of love for Neville and Sonia, there was so much he wanted to say to them, so much he felt he had to put right, although he thought he had always done his best for them. Everyone did the best they could in their own way . . . . everyone was evolving through many lifetimes of experience . . . . but sometimes the human way was difficult.

He emptied his lungs as he blew out a long, comfortable breath and patiently continued to contemplate his new vision . . . .

. . . . 'You have been sitting very thoughtfully for quite a while now George, can I be of any assistance to you?'

The voice startled George a little and he quickly brought his attention back into the Library. 'Oh yes . . . . I was miles away . . . . I was just thinking about our conversation and, err . . . . '

'Yes, I know you were thinking, I was helping you with your thoughts, and I have to say they are becoming very positive, a big change from the George of old.'

'Well, you have told me so much, opened my eyes to the poor state of the human mind. How could I not see that we need to think differently, need to take a close look at our way of living and do something about it? You have shown me it is necessary now for each individual to take responsibility for their actions and offer a change to the world.'

'Of course, your words are true, and I do hope our little talk has helped you to at least slow down a little and take a good look around. So much of life is taken for granted, so much effort is used up chasing the dreams and aspirations of the personality, so much thought is lost maintaining the hopes of a 'false self' which can never be satisfied.

If for one moment you can touch the true person behind your misgivings, if, for a second, you come across a feeling of expanded love that reaches out beyond the egoic self, your journey towards freedom has begun.

Don't forget - it is the evolutionary process. Through the negative you will find the positive. Through understanding what you are not, will you see what you are. I can assure you the *old* patterns, the *old* way of thinking and reacting to the conditioned habits you have acquired *will* change. Forgive what you do not understand, and know in your heart there is a purpose in everything you see.'

'Yes, I can appreciate that now, there is much about myself I am starting to question, a lot of things I do that suddenly make no sense to me.'

'Look at the words you speak, the intentions you hold, the ideas and beliefs that you build your world around. Notice your actions and interactions with others, your likes and dislikes, where your fears are coming from - it is all a part of recognising the truth of who you are, it is all a part of the beautiful game you call life.

You are a good man, George, with so much to give . . . . everyone has so much to give, but at the moment your morality is driven by society's influence. The way you have been taught to think has brought about a collapse of true virtue inwardly, and therefore has become a sad reflection of virtue outwardly. There is no love, there is no honesty, there is no passion for life because there is no freedom from the very structure of thought that has divided man from man, country from country. Now has come the time to find a new way before the old way has taken everything.

Morality is not put together by thought, it is not the outcome of political pressure or yesterday's tradition, morality is the outcome of love, and love is freedom from the violence of the mind.

A mind that is free and at peace realises it cannot be dependent on society's ideals. It sees clearly that to conform to such beliefs creates an inner conflict which again looks upon the world through fragmentations of anger, envy and selfishness. In short, life becomes a battle, driven on by the force of your fears.'

Listening to the voice speak these bold words, George could feel a recognition of truth, giving him a greater compassion for his fellow man. He felt a rising kinship, lifting him beyond the boundaries of his previous thinking; a belief that the world would become a better place when man could recognise his problem. To understand what the voice was saying seemed to release an intelligence in him that was more than thought, more than limited expectation.

'Freedom is a state of mind. It is not a momentary escape from something that is bothering you. This kind of freedom is a reaction to life, an immediate blotting out of circumstances and feelings that have hurt you, like the drug addict who constantly covers over the fear of living in pain, or the alcoholic who cannot face the burdens of life, this is purely freedom of escape but it is not permanent, it is not freedom from the mind.

Freedom comes when you see and act instantaneously, it cannot be sought and found through explanations and fashionable reasoning. Freedom is to see life without the blanket coverings of conformity and blind leadership. It is to look beyond the shallow thoughts of yesterday's mind and allow yourself the changes which have denied you the peace and love that you so desire. Freedom is the beauty of an innocent mind which is open to love.

But values and moral standards are starting to move in a positive direction after years and years of authoritative policing. The new world order is starting to turn, George, and you will become a big part of it, it is happening now as we speak.'

George smiled with a boyish glint in his eye as he acknowledged with a nod, the promise of a better world.

'As I have said, the greater change will not come from an outer revolution with violent intention, it will come when the mind has ceased to be divided, when there is an inner peace which cannot be ignored.'

'Yes, we must all try hard now to find that inner peace.'

'But remember this when you return to your earth life . . . . while ever you try and justify violence you cannot find peace, while ever you deny violence is the result of man's cultural and social heritage you cannot find peace. As you have discovered, one of the most common expressions of violence is anger, it is a rush of disturbed energy inside the emotional field which quite frequently leads to physical and verbal attack.

When you are annoyed by someone or insulted in the most ridiculous way, you say it is righteous to be angry. When your relationship has broken down leaving a financial hole in your life and you have to give up your possessions, you say it is justification for anger. When your country, your religion and way of life are under threat you are ready to fight for your freedom of belief, you are ready to send your children into battle to protect the ideals of your mind, and all this anger is said to be justified, morally righteous in the name of God or in the name of some other conceptual notion.

But when you take a closer look at anger, you will see it is a response to your fears, a way of manipulating life to justify your actions. You have to learn that to find a fundamental answer to your problems the mind has to be open to the truth, the mind has to become aware. There is no good or bad, only life and the experience it brings to you, this you have to know before you can move forward. You have to see that everything you condemn is an integral part of the inner consciousness you have made to separate yourself and justify the false image of who you are.

When you can see this and find love for each other at the deepest of levels, when you can release the conditioning that has created the false centre of 'me' and 'you', then all the division will come to an end. When you have reached the point of understanding that thought is the cause of separation and fear, it is a natural step for you to seek wholeness and love.

The human psyche needs stability and security, but unfortunately looks in the most unstable and insecure places and it is by paying great attention to these facts that the truth can be seen.'

'You mean attention to everything that causes distress?'

'I mean to be master of your mind requires great concentration and focused attention on whatever you are doing. It is easy for you here, George, to sit and listen to our conversation with a nod of approval - but it is a different matter for you to return to your earth life and put into practice all we have spoken about. The damage of conditioning is already stamped deep into the conscious behaviour of who you think you are, and without question, has left its mark on you as an individual *and* collectively. Until you can see this clearly and take action to free yourself from the tyranny of your thoughts, life will become no easier.

It does not matter how much knowledge you may try to understand, it does not matter which ideology, religion or cultural belief you may cast yourself into, it does not matter whether you sit under a tree and meditate for the rest of your days, or not . . . . . . what does matter, George, is the attention you can give to watching yourself closely, observing your every thought and seeing the true consequences of your mind action - but the good thing is, all of this I can now see you are ready to do.

You are all such beautiful souls lost into the content of your minds, living through a collection of thoughts that are misdirected. But I am with you, George, I am always with you, to give assistance and direction to everything you do in life. In your heart you will feel me, through love and understanding you will touch upon the truth of life with a guidance that may take you beyond all your fears.

There is a point you may reach when you become aware of my presence, a point where you are no longer seeking the security of your outer world, where your thoughts are no longer self-centred and are open to the oneness of everything. When you reach this point of awareness - even if it is just for one moment, you will see what has happened to the mind which has become so attentive. You will see it has become sensitive, not only mentally, but also physically. You will see it is silent and aware and is no longer seeking 'to be' anything at all. Yet out of this sensitivity it can act without breaking life up into separated fragments. It is a place of no fear, a moment when the true self is opening the heart to a real love which can unify the thoughts and feelings of everyone.

If you can find this place, then you will find a timeless state which is incredibly vast, a state you will seek to find again and again, until it is yours forever. It is a state that eventually all men will find, but it is a state that may only be achieved by looking at yourself. No ideology, no separatist belief, no cult or organisation can give you this . . . . it is something *you* have to do. This will bring about the release of the false self with its old conditioned ways of fear, and allow the resurgence of the true self, bringing with it a new quality of peace to the world.

And then one day I will ask you the question again: 'What is your story, George?' . . . . and you will answer: 'I am Love'.

. . . . An air of musky scent filled the vast recesses of the Library, a scent that seemed to hang everywhere; along the corridors, across the perfectly bound volumes neatly stacked upon the dark wooden shelves, down to the polished lattice of oaken flooring, stretching outwards and beyond where distance could not be recognised by human eyes. Drifting softly through the silence of the great hall, it lingered pleasantly around the perfectly arranged furniture of rosewood and mahogany, melting into the natural light that binds the Library to a place of serenity, a place of peace and comfort, knowledge and truth. Here, a mind could relax within a shelter where time had stopped; a retreat where silence was enough for everything the senses wanted to know.

. . . . As the silence fell, a great stillness moved softly across the Library, a stillness that cut through the air with a touch of graceful calm, a stillness that fell as a blessing of peace along the shelves and books to caress them with a whisper of love, as if a message of truth had fallen gently to throw its light upon a misguided soul.

George filled his lungs to wallow pleasantly in the glow of an immense passion for life, a passion which he believed had long since disappeared. He was alive again, swallowed up into the stillness of the room, breathing intensely into a rhythmical movement which pulled him readily beyond his thoughts, beyond his earthly desires, beyond his humanness.

He gently closed his eyes, the beat of his heart now embracing his whole body, effortlessly taking him deeper and deeper into his unconscious world, deeper and deeper into the place he wanted to be.

EPILOGUE

George partially opened his eyes, he squinted, blinking his eyelids to shield his sight from the annoyance of the flickering artificial light above his head. This wasn't the Library, he knew instinctively this was not the place he had felt so at ease and peaceful.

He could hear the sound of traffic echoing past in a dull monotonous tone. He could hear voices chattering in conversation close by; the muffled beep of a mobile phone sounding in someone's pocket; the rustling of newspapers and the chink of crockery. He could smell fried onions and bacon against the rich aroma of coffee, croissants and hot pastries blending into the drifting odours of cooking oil. The distinct smell of burned toast lifted into his nostrils, and he knew he was back . . . . he knew the Library had gone and he was back in the coffee shop.

Taking a deep breath he opened his eyes fully and looked around the room. The business men in striped suits were still here, as were the students with their brash hairstyles and gothic clothes. Over in the corner the two young girls were still giggling to each other, he remembered them all, as if nothing had ever happened.

George turned suddenly to look behind him and stared at the spotty-faced youth behind the counter, it was the same lad, shouting out the orders and frothing the cappuccinos. Everything was exactly as he had left it.

On the table in front of him, his coffee mug was next to his damp hat, he picked it up, it was half full and still steaming. He took a long, slow drink and returned it to the table with a realisation that this was it . . . . he was back on the earth.

He let out a slow stream of breath in relief of his deliverance and allowed himself a wry smile as he considered the peaceful, tranquil silence of the great Library, the beautiful smells that lingered around him in the most pleasant of ways, and yet . . . . he had chosen to return to this frantic world of continuous noise and unrest. But he was happy . . . . something inside him was bursting with happiness, jumping with an excitement he had not felt for years.

He lifted the mug to his lips again and swallowed another gulp of coffee, gazing intently around the room, basking in his new-found enthusiasm.

His stomach flipped as his thoughts quickly shifted to Phoebe, he suddenly felt very emotional as he realised he would soon be able to see her again. He had so much to tell her, so much to share with her. He so wanted to be with his family again. The voice had given him a lot to think about and he would try to get it right . . . . this was one thing he was sure of.

George raised his mug again, proudly straightening his back at the thought of his good intentions, and then gasped in disbelief as his eyes fell onto the bulging briefcase resting under the table by his feet. The interview! He had forgotten. He quickly wiped away the condensation from the steamed-up window and peered out through the murky drizzle, fixing his sight on the clock tower. Five to twelve! His plight was confirmed by a quick check of his watch and he felt a strange feeling of deja vu rising up inside.

George gulped down the last of his coffee, picked up his briefcase, planted his hat firmly on his head and dashed out into the street. Less than five minutes to cross Atlas Grove back to Wadsworth Road, collect the ticket and find his platform.

He increased his length of step, twisting and turning to avoid collision with the office workers, school kids and mothers with pushchairs.

At last, the subway station was clear in sight, only a few steps to cross the road . . . . he stepped from the footpath and then instinctively moved backwards as he heard the sharp ringtone of his mobile phone.

Maybe the car was speeding. George didn't know about that. Just a moment of anguish as the red Astra car screeched close to his rigid torso, missing him by inches. His lungs snatched for air as he stared in disbelief into the frightened, hollow eyes of the young driver. And then he was gone. With a surge of speed the car disappeared into the misty drizzle of Wadsworth Road.

George inhaled deeply, filling his lungs with the damp, heavy air, trying to calm himself and reached into his overcoat pocket for his phone. 'Yes . . . . George Eastwood speaking,' he breathed shakily into the phone.

'Oh yes, George, it's John Pullman here, from Waterloo Publishing . . . . how are you?'

'Well, err . . . . yes, yes I'm fine, John.' George pushed his finger in his other ear and moved further away from the busy road, surprised by the call. 'I'm just on my way to see you.'

'Yes, of course . . . . but that's why I'm calling, I was hoping to catch you in time. There's really no need for you to bother to come all this way today . . . . you see, we have already decided that you're the man we want for the job . . . . it's yours . . . . if you still want it, that is . . . .?'

'I certainly do!' George was quick to answer, a flicker of a smile spreading across his lips.

'Well that's good. Perhaps you could start next Monday . . . . shall we say nine o' clock at our offices, and we can discuss all the details then?'

'Yes . . . . yes, that's perfect. I'll be there at nine o' clock on Monday. Thank you so much for the call, John.'

'It's a pleasure, George. See you then . . . . bye now.'

'Bye . . . . bye.' George carefully pushed the phone back into his overcoat pocket, his head spinning with the good news.

He turned and shuffled slowly along the footpath, back towards the coffee shop, not really able to take everything in. What a day it had been. Certainly a day to remember.

Walking in a daze along the crescent of shops on Atlas Grove, he drifted past the Natwest Bank, glancing across at the bargain shops and bric-a-brac stores. Suddenly, he caught a glimpse of himself in a shop window, he smiled broadly and quickened his step, striding more intently now and briskly marched back into Wadsworth Road, a new purpose rising inside him.

He would go home . . . . home to Phoebe and start his life again. A childish excitement consumed his heart as he reached the tarmacadam driveways and the tree-planted grass verges. On and on he walked, battling the dismal elements, majestically reaching out towards his destination. He glanced upward into the overcast heavens and breathed deeply, allowing his sight to fall onto the short distance between his solitary figure and his home, clearly in full view now amidst the greyness of the day.

His heart swelled with an openness of passion and love, beating harmoniously to his rhythmical movement, closer and closer, step by step, little by little, back towards his world. He thought once again of the voice and everything they had spoken of and smiled knowingly to himself.

Switching his briefcase to his other hand, George kicked a pile of wet leaves high into the air as the swirling wind blew them back into his glowing face. 'I'm coming home, Phoeb,' he spoke the words softly from deep within his heart, ' . . . . at last, I'm coming home.'

THE LAST WORD

These days, when I look out from my window, I see a different world. Not that too much has changed, although times are certainly changing. Changing in a way that, on the surface, may not seem too different, but on the inside, the human race has become more aware. Not only of the way the world operates, which in itself has become a drudgery of material gain and technological development, but a stretching out of the senses to look beyond the high flying revolution of the 90's and new millennium, to a more positive viewpoint of simplicity. A more open perspective and innocent perception that looks around with awareness at the destruction of our environment, the greed and inhospitable nature of man's arrogance and stature upon the earth.

Although we still hold strongly onto the vast governmental issues and banking systems that control the strings of finance within their firm grip, and yes, we still fall short when it comes to practicing an openness and affection for each other beyond our special group of friends and relationships, now, at least a consciousness has taken shape, which by its very nature, can only grow, as we become more open to a new order of living within the world.

Industries will take new form as working conditions and hours of work change. Governments must now, at last, become aware that the people no longer will stand for the traditional blunders that so often have plagued the earth with wars and famines, exploitation and greed. These things we have become aware of, and only with this new consciousness can the problems be solved.

Political systems must open their eyes to create a better way of life. Media machines driven for manipulation and political gain will no longer be used to control the thinking of the people. Education will have to reconsider the old fashioned process of pointing our children towards a class system that promotes bitterness and self-criticism, loss of confidence and poor self-esteem.

Many things must change for this world to survive. Many things must be looked upon in a different light for the human race to progress and evolve.

Parents must look at the way they raise their children, with a new vision of humility and compassion to fit the new purpose of a changing society, a community where helping others is paramount in our daily lives, where honesty and truthfulness stretch before us as a guiding beacon of light.

We speak of freedom, but are bound by the chains of our fears. We speak of love, but are chastised by the needs and expectations of our humanism. Our greed and superfluous lifestyle has taken us to the edge of despair, where twisted minds, tired from the search for external happiness, are now laid heavy in confusion, which may only be lifted by a change of vision. A change which can only be affected by looking beyond all we have created, and knowing who we truly are.

At this point in time there is a great need to look inward, and recognise that, as individuals, *we* are responsible for the global disaster we see before us. *We are the world* and it is the correction of our own internal chaos which will shine a light of truth on the disorder of our outer world.

There is a voice inside all of us that speaks beyond the confusion that has become our world. All we need do is listen . . . . after all, it is only our thoughts that separate us from each other and a place of everlasting love.

George.

ABOUT THE AUTHOR

Let us introduce ourselves. We are Michael and Lynda Goodwin and for many years now we have been following the feelings of our hearts which have taken us to a greater depth of knowledge and spiritual enlightenment. It has been through this personal evolution that the writing of 'Whatever Happened to George?' was inspired, with the greatest of wishes to help develop the light of spiritually in others.

With consideration for the natural changes that Mother Earth is bringing about and with the lighter energies from the universe already upon us, it is our great desire to assist in the exciting spiritual revolution in the best way we know how.

We made the choice to retire from work at a relatively early age, now being 60 and 59 respectively, and have recently moved home to the Yorkshire Dales National Park. Michael is a keen amateur musician and lyricist, Lynda's passion is painting, especially in oils. Walking and exercising has become part of our daily routine. We have been married for 28 years and have one daughter and two granddaughters.